THE
MINISTRY
OF QUIZZES

David Gentle has been a consultant, an engineer and a marketeer, travelling from Baku (the world's lowest-lying capital city, at 28m below sea level) to Tokyo (the only capital that is an anagram of the city it superseded). But the one true constant has been his love of trivia. He is the author of *On the Tip of My Tongue*, the popular quiz book (or *apex linguae* to a medic). He lives in the UK near Bath (where Mary Shelley completed *Frankenstein* and William Herschel discovered Uranus) with his much-quizzed wife and two sons. His ambition is to one day write the perfect quiz question, and, with more than 10,000 attempts to date, feels he is nearing (to quote a certain British prime minister) the end of the beginning.

(It's Kyoto, if you were wondering.)

To Peter Gentle, the kindest, cleverest man I have known.

Also by David Gentle

On the Tip of My Tongue

THE
MINISTRY
OF QUIZZES

David Gentle

PAN BOOKS

First published in trade paperback 2021 by Macmillan

This edition published 2022 by Pan Books
an imprint of Pan Macmillan
The Smithson, 6 Briset Street, London EC1M 5NR
EU representative: Macmillan Publishers Ireland Ltd, 1st Floor
The Liffey Trust Centre, 117–126 Sheriff Street Upper,
Dublin 1, D01 YC43
Associated companies throughout the world
www.panmacmillan.com

ISBN 978-1-5290-8712-3

1 3 5 7 9 8 6 4 2

A CIP catalogue record for this book is available from the British Library.

Design layout by Carrdesignstudio.com
Typeset by Carrdesignstudio.com
Printed and bound by CPI Group (UK) Ltd, Croydon, CRO 4YY

Visit **www.panmacmillan.com** to read more about all our books
and to buy them. You will also find features, author interviews and
news of any author events, and you can sign up for e-newsletters
so that you're always first to hear about our new releases.

♔ THE MINISTRY OF QUIZZES

Deep in the heart of Whitehall, up an unnoticeable side road, is an unassuming office block. Unremarkable on the outside, inside it buzzes and bustles with activity. Civil servants hard at work – researching, compiling, cross-checking facts and trivia, questions and puzzles. This is *The Ministry of Quizzes*.

Formed by the 1957 Quizzing and Puzzling Act, from a merger between the Board of General Knowledge and the Office of Quizmasters, this small but essential government department is the national authority on all matters relating to quizzes, trivia and puzzles. Often overlooked, operating in the shadow of the other great offices of state, the officials of this curious and little-known corner of government work diligently and tirelessly to carry out the vital work of documenting, processing, vetting and overseeing all the nation's quiz-related affairs.

Now for the first time, their work can be revealed.

The author was given unique access by officials, observing their day-to-day operations, sitting in on their committees and reviewing and analyzing their copious output. He was shown the inner workings of the Ministry, and the actions and activities of the Ministry's various sub-departments. The Office for Connections, Sequences and Other Coincidences, whose brief is to investigate and discover patterns and relationships between facts. The Secretariat of Specialist Topics, who research and categorize specific areas of general knowledge. Even the secretive Office of Enigmas, Conundrums and Other Devious Puzzles, who preside over some of the department's most perplexing problem-setting.

This book is the result. A comprehensive, varied and in-depth compilation of the fascinating work of this enigmatic and much-loved national institution.

👑 HOW IT WORKS

The officials of The Ministry of Quizzes are sticklers for rules and process. But the main advice on how to use this book is not to follow any particular method and navigate as you wish. Just don't tell the Ministry that.

The book is a compendium of different formats of quizzes and puzzles, each with a reference to its set of answers in the back. There is no particular sequence or order; the different quizzes are evenly distributed throughout the book. So is the difficulty of questions. If you are already tearing your hair out at page one, at least be comforted that the questions won't get any harder.

Quizzes are always better played with others! If you are in a group – whether you're on holiday, gathered around a dinner table or just down the pub – have a pencil and paper to hand and appoint someone as quizmaster. Decide in advance how many rounds you will play. Scoring suggestions are included with the answers to each set of questions. Alternatively, make up your own games.

You can play the book on your own, of course, and you'll find some of the quiz formats are well suited to solo play. And you are welcome to browse and harvest the questions for your own quizzes.

Care has been taken with each of the 1,837 questions in this book, but inevitably, even with the resources of the Ministry, amid this quantity of information factual inaccuracies can appear. Errors can creep in through the passage of time, debatable or disputed subject matter or just plain . . . ahem. In this event, the policy of the Ministry is to offer a full and frank apology, and do everything possible to avoid an independent enquiry.

👑 ABOUT THE QUIZZES

The relationship between quiz-setter and quiz-solver is not always an easy one. Difficult questions can alienate an audience. But make them too easy and there is no challenge and little reward. The problem for the quiz-setter is that knowledge is binary – you either know the answer or you don't. And what is 'hard' varies from person to person, and depending on the type of quiz. A question an individual may struggle with can be easy pickings for a quiz team. Nothing, of course, beats the satisfaction of being the only person, or only team, to get the question right. But the Goldilocks quiz question – not too hard, not too easy – is an elusive thing.

The ideal quiz question sits somewhere at this boundary between knowledge and ignorance. A perfect quiz question would be possible to answer even if you have never come across the subject before, either by using background knowledge, or through information in the question itself. Good quiz questions should entertain and inform. If the answer is interesting or surprising in some way – or even annoying – if a new neural pathway gets connected, that in itself is a pleasing thing.

This book is designed with these thoughts in mind. Some of the quiz formats will be familiar, some less so. Some are more devious than others. But help can come from unexpected quarters. Often the quizzes offer ways to get to the answer even when your memory banks have turned up blank. The best way to discover the world of the Ministry of Quizzes is, of course, to dive in and play. But here are some musings, up front, on what you can expect to find:

Many of the quiz formats in the book have linked answers – that is, the answers are connected or share something in common. Examples are the 'Connections' and 'Linkophilia' quizzes. These give you alternative ways of completing the quiz, and confirming, or working back to questions you previously couldn't answer. In the case of Linkophilia, this is similar to completing a crossword, in that you build information that helps you as you go.

The same principle applies to 'Magic Square'. Magic Squares originated in ancient China and have a long history. Essentially a grid of numbers, the rows, columns and diagonals in a Magic Square add up to the same number, giving it an arcane and mythical status in many civilizations and cultures since. Applied by the Ministry of Quizzes, it means you can use arithmetic to bridge gaps in knowledge and, if successful, eventually answer all the questions. Other grid-based formats, 'Cluedoku' and 'Letter Box', follow a similar principle.

The 'Picture Logic' quizzes are in a similar vein. Rather than asking the obvious 'who or what is this picture of?', the questions ask about things related to the pictures or groups of pictures within the set. Think of them as clues. By comparing different questions you may find you can make educated guesses about the pictures you don't know, helping you to discover their identities.

In some of the formats, the links are in the question content itself. 'In Common', 'What Comes Next?' and 'Odd One Out' formats are all about being able to spot patterns in the data. Often these call for lateral thinking. Be warned, these quizzes contain some of the Ministry's most devious and infuriating questions.

There is history behind another of the formats – 'The Wisdom of the Crowd'. In 1906, Francis Galton, a scientist and relation of Charles Darwin, received an unexpected insight at a country fair in Plymouth. Observing a guess-the-weight-of-the-ox competition at the show, Galton made the surprising discovery that by taking the median (or middle) guess from 800 entry tickets, the crowd's result was accurate to within 1 per cent of the true weight. This was far better than any single expert at the show. This idea is taken up by the Ministry of Quizzes, putting similar 'guess the quantity'-type questions to people up and down the country. In each case the crowd's data is set out. Can you use this to find the correct answer? How many of the crowd will you beat in the process?

The Ministry of Quizzes likes anagrams, and you'll find they are liberally sprinkled throughout this book. Anagrams can be tricky, but they have the obvious benefit that the answer can always be found in the question. Many of the anagram questions are in a similar format to those you might find in a cryptic crossword. A sentence that disguises three parts: the anagram text itself that needs to be rearranged, a description of what the answer is, and the two linked by an indicator word like 'reordered' or 'turned into'. To help you, these questions are tagged with (anag, x), where x is the number of letters in the answer.

Other than anagrams, there are no other cryptic-crossword-type questions.

There are a host of other question formats in the book that may be more familiar.

General Knowledge is the bread and butter of quizzing, and there is a plentiful mix of formats, from direct questions to multiple-choice questions. In the 'Four Clues' quiz, you are given clues in turn to a person, thing, event, place or date. The challenge is to get to the answer by using the minimum number of clues. So, try to take one clue at a time and not to skim ahead. With 'Matching Pairs' you are trying to link pairs of things together – for instance historic events and the people connected with them. For a more challenging game you can play 'blind' by covering the second set of the pairs and earn more points.

Some of the formats are concerned with lists of things. 'Put in Order', as the name suggests, asks you to arrange a list in a correct order . . . for instance, planets according to size, or historical events in chronological order. And scattered across the book is a format of question that asks you to name items from a list of ten things from a common category. You can make as many guesses as you like; correct answers gain points, but wrong answers lose them. Obscure answers earn more points.

Everyone has their favourite areas of knowledge and specialist subject, so the Ministry also provides a set of quizzes that focus in on specific areas of knowledge. Science, the arts, history, pop culture, sport, geography and many more are catered for, giving the perfect opportunity for you to shine in your pet subject (or to keep a low profile).

Finally, to give the quiz-solver the best possible odds, there is the 'Fifty-Fifty' format and its close cousin 'More, Less or the Same?' It's a straight choice. A correct answer is no harder than predicting the toss of a coin. How hard can that be? So why do these rounds seem to provoke so much tension in the audience?

On behalf of the Ministry of Quizzes, I hope you enjoy this book as much as I have enjoyed writing it. Use it in the way that suits you best – whether to play the quizzes solo, with friends or family, to use them to set your own quizzes, or inspire you to come up with new questions and formats. You may even be just what the Ministry is looking for, and a career in Whitehall beckons . . .

Enjoy your quizzing!

David Gentle

👑 ACKNOWLEDGEMENTS

It is impossible to thank everyone who has helped this book become a physical reality. But there are some to whom I am particularly indebted.

Thank you to everyone at Pan Macmillan, and especially to Rachel Feebery and Rebecca Needes, and to my brilliant editor, Matthew Cole. Thank you to Helena Caldon for your forensic reviewing skills and to Vanessa Maynard for your ideas for the original design. Thank you to Niall Harman and all at Curtis Brown, and a big thank you to Gordon Wise for your advice and ideas, effort, and belief.

Thank you to everyone who has, inadvertently or otherwise, inspired ideas for questions, especially to Alex Gentle, Eve Dudley, Florence Hollands, James Miller, Jonathan Derwent, Ric Dudley and Zac Gentle.

A special thank you to my very own 'Man at the Ministry', Jules Kirby, for inspiring the title.

Thank you to all my friends in the 'Quarantini Quiz' for unknowingly road-testing many of the questions and formats. I'm sorry I couldn't include more country outlines.

Thank you to Louisa Nelson for being an inspiration.

Thank you to Pamela Gentle and Helen Miller for your never-ending love and support.

And finally, a huge thank you to Zac, Alex and Kate Gentle, for being the best sounding-board, for tolerating my absences at the computer when there was football to be played and wine to be drunk, and not least all your happy encouragement.

CONTENTS

THE QUIZZES

ANSWERS

THE
QUIZZES

👑 FIRSTS

These questions concern notorious 'firsts'. How many can you answer?

1. What was the first James Bond novel?
2. The first televised address from the Oval Office was made in 1947, by which president?
3. On 16 May 1975, Junko Tabei of Japan became the first woman to do what?
4. What first was achieved by Rachael Blackmore in 2021?
5. By what title is the First Lord of the Treasury in the UK better known?
6. Hattie McDaniel was the first African-American to win an Oscar, for her performance in which film?
7. What is significant about a goal scored by Lucien Laurent of France against Mexico on 13 July 1930?
8. Julia Gillard was the first female prime minister of which country?
9. *A Study in Scarlet* was the first story to feature which character?
10. What watery feat was Captain Matthew Webb the first to do, in 1875?

Find the answers on page 223.

👑 COUNTRIES BORDERING BRAZIL

Try to name the **10** countries that border Brazil. Earn points for more obscure answers, lose points for incorrect answers.

The answers are on page 219.

Try to answer these miscellaneous questions.

1. Leon Spinks did it in 1978, Ken Norton in 1973 and Joe Frazier in 1971. What?

2. What links Lisa del Giocondo and Kate Winslet?

3. Some languages, such as Nigerian, have a 'hesternal' tense, for describing events that occur specifically when?

4. How are Haven Brow, Short Brow, Rough Brow, Brass Point, Flagstaff Point, Baily's Hill and Went Hill Brow collectively known?

5. In the Harry Potter series, what honour is given to witches and wizards for great accomplishments?

6. If New York is the Big Apple, which US city is the 'Mini Apple'?

7. How would you write 950 in Roman numerals?

8. Bio valuers succumbing to this dangerous, infectious microbe? (anag, 5,5)

9. What is an ANPR system used to identify?

10. 'Fear Tech' is the rival to which other fictional academic institution?

11. 'This blessed plot, this earth, this realm, this England.' Which play?

12. What catastrophic event ends an 'antediluvian' period?

13. What literary first is accorded to the 1995 book *Fluid Concepts and Creative Analogies* by Douglas Hofstadter?

14. Which outlaw has been played by Ray Winstone, Christian Slater and Scott Grimes?

15. Which pasta dish gets its name from the Italian for 'charcoal burner'?

The answers are on page 215.

⚜ THE WISDOM OF THE CROWD: UK CITIES

The Ministry of Quizzes asked 200 people in the UK: *'How many cities are there in the UK?'* This is how they responded:

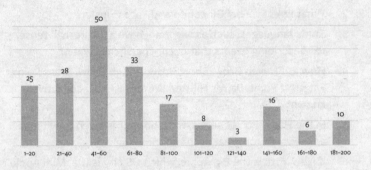

	1–20	21–40	41–60	61–80	81–100	101–120	121–140	141–160	161–180	181–200
	25	28	50	33	17	8	3	16	6	10

(For instance, 25 people gave an answer in the range of 1 and 20.*)

The middle answer **60**	The most popular answer **50**	The average answer **74**
59	**65**	**60**	**69**
The middle answer from people aged over 30	The middle answer from people aged 30 or under	The most popular answer from people from the North	The most popular answer from people from the South

Based on this data, or otherwise, what is *your* estimate of the number of cities in the UK?

The answer is on page 211.

* 4 people answered 'don't know'; their responses have not been included.

👑 TREES

These questions are all related to trees. How many can you answer?

1. The largest forest in England is in which county?
2. Which popular US ski resort takes its name from the trees that grow around it?
3. Saucy letup shaken up a tree? (anag, 10)
4. What gas do trees take in from the atmosphere when they photosynthesize?
5. What two-word phrase links Anton Chekhov and AFC Bournemouth?
6. The active ingredient of aspirin is found in the bark of which tree?
7. What do larches do in autumn that is unusual for conifers?
8. Which country is named after a tree?
9. Xylem is a woody structure that transports what up through a tree?
10. Which tree is traditionally found in British churchyards?

The answers are on page 208.

👑 ODD ONE OUT 1

Which is the odd one out in each of these lists, and why?

1. Quakers, Shakers, Pilgrims, Mormons.
2. Dartmoor, Bodmin Moor, North York Moors, Exmoor.
3. Nurse, Sister, Matron, Doctor.
4. Garlic, Ginger, Wasabi, Horseradish.
5. Coney Island, Isle of Purbeck, Malta, Holy Island of Lindisfarne.

The answers are on page 203.

Try to pick the correct answer from the choices given:

1. In *The Gruffalo*, which creature does the mouse meet first?
   - **A.** Snake
   - **B.** Owl
   - **C.** Fox
   - **D.** Gruffalo

2. Which country had a civil war from 1946 to 1949?
   - **A.** Greece
   - **B.** Hungary
   - **C.** Japan
   - **D.** Spain

3. Norwich in 1959 was the first UK city to have a what?
   - **A.** Bypass
   - **B.** Postcode
   - **C.** ATM
   - **D.** Telephone exchange

4. Which state does Hannah Montana come from?
   - **A.** Montana
   - **B.** Tennessee
   - **C.** California
   - **D.** Texas

5. 'Every action has an equal and opposite reaction' is which of Newton's Laws?
   - **A.** First
   - **B.** Second
   - **C.** Third
   - **D.** Fourth

6. Which is NOT an ingredient of Worcestershire Sauce?
   - **A.** Anchovies
   - **B.** Garlic
   - **C.** Molasses
   - **D.** Tomatoes

The answers are on page 199.

♛ FIFTY-FIFTY I

Try to answer these fifty-fifty questions.

1. Which is in the Northern Hemisphere, the **Tropic of Cancer** or the **Tropic of Capricorn**?
2. What is the UK's bestselling flavour of soup, **chicken** or **tomato**?
3. What is the last word of James Joyce's *Ulysses*, **Yes** or **No**?
4. What is the collective word for crows, a **murder** or a **parliament**?
5. Who is older, **Gary Oldman** or **Gary Numan**?

The answers are on page 195.

♛ CONNECTIONS I

The answers to these questions share a link . . . can you work out what it is?

1. What organization, created by the United Nations General Assembly in 1946, provides support for the health and well-being of children around the world?
2. Where was Marco Polo born?
3. What title, meaning literally 'in place of the king', describes an official who runs a country, province or colony in the name of the monarch?
4. What was the name of the series of books that feature 'autostereograms', graphics that allow people to see hidden 3D images?
5. Which dinosaur of the Late Cretaceous period has a name derived from Greek, meaning 'three-horned face'?

What is the connection that the answers have in common?

Find out on page 191.

These questions refer to the symbols pictured. Some questions may give you clues to the answers to others. Use this – and your knowledge, of course – to work out as many of their meanings as you can . . . and answer the questions.

1. Which *two* warn of chemical hazards?
2. Which *three* concern laundry care?
3. Which *two* are used on technology devices?
4. Which relates to biology?
5. Which *two* represent political movements?
6. Which *two* represent horoscopes?
7. Which *two* are map symbols?
8. Which *two* relate to drying of laundry?
9. Which relates to wireless connectivity?
10. Which is a chemical hazard – and a Britney Spears song?
11. Which relates to bleaching of laundry?
12. Which means 'recycled'?
13. Which means 'recyclable'?
14. Which *two* are opposite sexes?
15. Which is concerned with al fresco eating?
16. Which means beach, and which might be found on the beach?

The solution is on page 187.

A.

B.

C.

D.

E.

F.

G.

H.

I.

J.

K.

L.

M.

N.

O.

P.

Try to answer these miscellaneous questions:

1. 'I don't care what they're going to say / Let the storm rage on.' What line comes next?
2. Which continent makes up 6 per cent of the Earth's surface?
3. Which football team was founded in 1895 as the works team of the Thames Iron Works?
4. Which capital city sits on the River Spree?
5. Which iconic building is known as Torre Pendente in its local language?
6. What does the 'A' of DNA stand for?
7. *Three Men on the Bummel* was the sequel to which popular novel?
8. In internet slang, what does TLDR stand for?
9. What international agreement signed in Poland in May 1955 was officially known as the 'Treaty of Friendship, Cooperation and Mutual Assistance'?
10. How is the artist Doménikos Theotokópoulos of the late Renaissance better known?
11. What brand is promoted by Cornelius Rooster?
12. What anagram of 'Rasputin' would most likely not approve of his licentious lifestyle?
13. In netball, which player restarts the game after a goal has been scored?
14. Between 1937 and 1964, which bridge was the longest in the world?
15. Who plays the title character in *Killing Eve*?

The answers are on page 223.

The clues correspond to single letters. The letters make a coiled-up, 9-letter word or name. The word can start in any square, and can run in any direction, but always through adjacent squares. Solve the clues and unscramble the word.

Clue: An artist . . .

Jay	Major Boothroyd	UN Secretary General Thant
ISO 216 paper sizes	Mark left by Don Diego de La Viego	River flowing into Loch Mohr
Fifty Romans	Vehicle identifier for Spain	SI unit of potential difference

The solution is on page 207.

The solution is on page 207.

👑 WHAT COMES NEXT? 1

Who or what comes next in each of these sequences?

1. Oklahoma, New Mexico, Arizona, Alaska . . .?
2. Bernard Lee, Robert Brown, Edward Fox, Judi Dench . . .?
3. Lygos, Byzantium, Augusta Antonina, Constantinople . . .?
4. William Shakespeare, Michael Faraday, Edward Elgar, Adam Smith . . .?
5. COA, AB, JS, AOC, CH . . .?

The answers are on page 215.

Find each answer using the clues in turn – the least number of clues the better.

1. Who is this?
   - His grandfather was Harald 'Bluetooth' Gormsson, of whom the wireless connectivity technology was named.
   - His father was Sweyn Forkbeard, king of Denmark from 986 to 1014.
   - He was king of England from 1016 to 1035.
   - Legend has it that he set his throne on the beach and commanded the tide to turn.

2. What is this?
   - It was discovered by Hennig Brand, an alchemist, around 1669, from experiments with human urine.
   - It is a key ingredient in DNA and RNA molecules and in ATP, a molecule that cells use to store energy.
   - Its name comes from Greek, meaning 'light bearer'.
   - Its chemical symbol is P.

3. Where is this?
   - La Navidad, founded by Columbus, and the first European settlement in the Americas, was founded in this modern country.
   - It is one of two countries sharing the island of Hispaniola.
   - It became sovereign in 1804 and the first country in the world to abolish slavery.
   - The country was devastated by an earthquake in 2010.

The answers are on page 211.

♛ CHOICE OF FOUR 2

Try to pick the correct answers for these questions:

1. In Minecraft, obsidian is made by mixing what?
   - **A.** Wood and iron
   - **B.** Iron and lava
   - **C.** Water and diamonds
   - **D.** Water and lava

2. What part of the brain gets its name from its resemblance to the shape of a sea horse?
   - **A.** Cerebellum
   - **B.** Hypothalamus
   - **C.** Hippocampus
   - **D.** Cerebral cortex

3. The Stars and Stripes has the most stars (50) of any national flag. Which nation's flag has the second most stars?
   - **A.** Venezuela
   - **B.** Kosovo
   - **C.** Australia
   - **D.** Brazil

4. Who is the title character of *The Merchant of Venice*?
   - **A.** Antonio
   - **B.** Shylock
   - **C.** Malvolio
   - **D.** Iago

5. Who was the ringleader of the Gunpowder Plot?
   - **A.** Thomas Percy
   - **B.** Robert Catesby
   - **C.** Francis Tresham
   - **D.** Guido Fawkes

6. In *Guardians of the Galaxy*, who supplies the voice of Rocket Raccoon?
   - **A.** Bradley Cooper
   - **B.** George Clooney
   - **C.** Chris Rock
   - **D.** Ryan Reynolds

Find the answers on page 207.

The clues in the grid correspond to numbers. The rows, columns and the two diagonals add up to the same number – the Magic Number. Use the clues to find this Magic Number and solve the grid!

Clue to the Magic Number: Location of a seasonal miracle.

Spots on a *Twister* mat	*Gentlemen of Verona*	Tighthead prop	Tent hire (anag.)
Tudor monarchs (non-disputed)	Spinal Tap's amp goes to . . .	Points on Mohs scale of hardness	Countries bordering Austria
Heads on a hydra	Zone 1 London tube stations beginning with 'B'	Feet in a fathom	*Angry Men*
Smallest composite number	Atomic number of silicon	Known paintings by Leonardo da Vinci	UK number ones by Iron Maiden

The solution is on page 202.

Arrange the items in each of these lists in the correct order.

1. Starting in the North and going south, put these UK cities in order of location.

   - Grimsby
   - Lancaster
   - St Albans
   - Swindon
   - Leicester

2. Put these lines from 'Bohemian Rhapsody' in order of when they appear for the first time in the song.

   - 'Beelzebub has a devil put aside for me'
   - 'Galileo Figaro'
   - 'Mama, just killed a man'
   - 'Can't do this to me, baby'
   - 'Is this the real life?'

3. Starting with the least, put these molecules in order of how many atoms they each have.

   - Ethanol
   - Sulphuric acid
   - Salt
   - Caffeine
   - Water

4. Starting with the fewest, what is the correct order of these Christmas gifts?

   - Pipers piping
   - French hens
   - Ladies dancing
   - Maids a-milking
   - Swans a-swimming

The answers are on page 199.

👑 HIP HOP AND RAP

These questions are all on the topic of hip hop and rap. How many can you answer?

1. How is rapper Mathangi 'Maya' Arulpragasam better known?
2. Which rapper had '99 Problems'?
3. Dr. Dre, Ice Cube and DJ Yella were members of which group?
4. Which rapper headlined Glastonbury in 2019?
5. Lauryn Hill was a member of which group?
6. Which rapper interrupted Taylor Swift's acceptance speech at the 2009 MTV Music Awards?
7. Who wrote the lyric 'Better late than never but never late is better'?
8. How is Curtis James Jackson III better known?
9. Who had a 2010 UK number one with 'Pass Out', a song that also featured in the opening ceremony of the 2012 Olympics?
10. 'I'll be Missing you' featuring Puff Daddy, Faith Evans and 112, and which sampled 'Every Breath You Take' by The Police was written in memory of which murdered rapper?

The answers are on page 195.

👑 WHAT COMES NEXT? 2

Who or what comes next in each of these sequences?

1. The Shard, Canary Wharf, NatWest Tower, The Post Office Tower, Millbank Tower . . .?
2. Love, Goodbye, Madonna, Jude, Back . . .?
3. Helsinki, Melbourne, Rome, Tokyo, Mexico City . . .?
4. *Little Britain*, Boxing Ring, Middle Ages, Stock Index . . .
5. P, TP, TOAK, S, F, FH . . .?

The answers are on page 191.

Try to answer these miscellaneous questions:

1. What is aibohphobia (apparently) the fear of?
2. Before she died in England on 31 May 2009, Millvina Dean had been the oldest living survivor of what?
3. What is the subject of Renoir's painting *Les Parapluies*?
4. In astrophysics, what is a SMBH?
5. If you were visiting the Winter Palace of Bogd Khan in the city of Ulaanbaatar, what country would you be in?
6. What word links Givanildo Vieira de Sousa, Terry Gene Bollea and Mark Ruffalo?
7. On the internet, what number appears if the page is not found?
8. What was the codename of the military operation to liberate Kuwait in 1990?
9. Paint alone to make this Italian ice cream? (anag, 10)
10. Eratosthenes was the first person to calculate the size of what?
11. Which Norfolk town gained its current name in 1537 when the Crown took it over from the Church?
12. On a standard keyboard, what is unusual about the keys F and J?
13. The protagonist in which novel describes himself as 'a mathematician with some behavioural difficulties'?
14. Which word for a type of pastry means 'whirlpool' in German?
15. What is the main ingredient of kimchi?

The answers are on page 187.

The clues in the grid relate to the numbers 1 to 9. No number is repeated. Use a process of elimination to work out which number is which.

A brace	Reign of Lady Jane Grey in days	UK number ones by Oasis
Novels by George Eliot	Tombliboos	Dialling code for the US
Category of most destructive hurricane	Equal to its number of letters	Degrees of separation

Go to page 223 for the solution.

What do the terms in each of these lists have in common?

1. Black, Sulu, Coral, Irish, Ross.
2. Hustle, connection, job, prisoner, patient.
3. Old, little, mutual, hard, great.
4. Tim Smit (founder of the Eden Project), Sara Baras (flamenco dancer), Mark Kram (sports writer), Ordelafo Faledro (the 34th Doge of Venice).
5. Naked, high, jacket, last, continental.

The answers are on page 219.

👑 THE ORCHESTRA

How many questions related to the orchestra can you answer?

1. Which instrument in the orchestra traditionally supplies the tuning note?
2. What does 'tutti' mean in the context of an orchestra?
3. Which instrument is played by the leader of the brass section?
4. What is a musical composition, generally in three parts, where a soloist is accompanied by an orchestra?
5. Which composer's work, 'Das Rheingold', called for six harps?
6. Who conducted the London Symphony Orchestra at the opening ceremony of the 2012 Olympics?
7. What word, related to the orchestra, means 'music loving'?
8. Which composer's work was central to the Morecambe and Wise sketch with André Previn?
9. How is Elgar's 'Variation IX' better known?
10. With what instrument is Jacqueline du Pré associated?

The answers are on page 215.

👑 CONNECTIONS 2

The answers to these questions have a common link . . . what is it?

1. What did Gwyneth Paltrow and Chris Martin name their first child?
2. Which BBC sitcom of the 1980s featured the Boswell family?
3. In which English county are Kidderminster, the Vale of Evesham and the Malvern Hills?
4. What is the two-letter postcode for the Hemel Hempstead area?
5. How is the *mentha* genus of plants commonly known?

What connection do these answers share?

Find out if you are right on page 198.

Try to pick the correct answers to each of these questions:

1. 'This is the night mail crossing the border / Bringing the cheque and the postal order . . .' Which poet wrote 'The Night Mail'?

   A. John Betjeman   **B.** W. H. Auden

   C. E. E. Cummings   **D.** Samuel Beckett

2. Which of these classical styles of architecture is the most recent?

   A. Corinthian   **B.** Doric

   C. Ionic   **D.** Tuscan

3. The word 'muscle' comes from the Latin word for which animal?

   A. Mosquito   **B.** Mollusc

   C. Moose   **D.** Mouse

4. How long is 'Bohemian Rhapsody'?

   A. 4 minutes 55 seconds   **B.** 5 minutes 25 seconds

   C. 5 minutes 55 seconds   **D.** 6 minutes 25 seconds

5. Which does NOT produce its own bank notes?

   A. Jersey   **B.** Gibraltar

   C. Isle of Man   **D.** Wales

6. Which of these team positions is the odd one out?

   A. Goal Shooter   **B.** Shooting Guard

   C. Goal Defence   **D.** Goal Attack

The answers are on page 211.

👑 MORE, LESS OR THE SAME? 1

Which of these is more, which is less . . . or are they the same?

1. Which has more carbon atoms, a molecule of **carbon monoxide**, or a molecule of **carbon dioxide**? Or are they the same?

2. Not including overseas territories, which has more borders with other countries, **Germany** or **France**? Or are they the same?

3. Who was older (in years) when they died, **Princess Diana** or **Marilyn Monroe**? Or were they the same age?

4. Which of these slang terms for money is worth more, a **Deep-Sea Diver** or a **Pavarotti**? Or are they the same?

5. Who has had more UK number one singles, **Little Mix** or **One Direction**? Or are they the same?

The answers are on page 219.

👑 FIFTY-FIFTY 2

Try to answer these fifty-fifty questions.

1. What was advertised with the slogan: 'It comes from paradise and tastes like heaven', **Bounty** or **Malibu**?

2. Which lies further east, **New York City** or **Santiago, Chile**?

3. In the musical *West Side Story*, which is the Puerto Rican gang, the **Sharks** or the **Jets**?

4. Who received more red cards at senior level (in league and international appearances), **Wayne Rooney** or **David Beckham**?

5. What type of creature is Sebastian, who sings 'Under the Sea' in *The Little Mermaid*, a **crab** or a **lobster**?

Answers on page 202.

👑 ODD ONE OUT 2

Which is the odd one out in each of these lists, and why?

1. *Wuthering Heights, The Tenant of Wildfell Hall, Jane Eyre, Mansfield Park*
2. Cannelloni, Linguini, Ravioli, Tortellini
3. Monica, Rachel, Emily, Carol
4. Dushanbe, Kinshasa, Dar es Salaam, Abuja
5. Reef knot, fisherman's knot, rolling hitch, sheet bend

The answers are on page 198.

👑 RAILWAY STATIONS WITH THREE-LETTER NAMES

Try to list the **10** UK railway stations with three-letter names. Earn points for more obscure answers, lose points for incorrect answers.

Turn to page 194 for the answers.

👑 IN COMMON 2

What do the terms in each of these lists have in common?

1. Edward Nigma, Oswald Chesterfield Cobblepot, Selina Kyle, Harvey Dent.
2. Emma Bunton, Anthony Kiedis, Dolores O'Riordan, will.i.am.
3. Beef, Wall, Syndrome, Sling, Rose.
4. Fiddle, steak, finest, May, Fashion.
5. Washington State, Édouard Manet, Kensington, Statue of Zeus.

Turn to page 191 for the answers.

Find each answer using the clues in turn – the least number of clues the better.

1. When (what year) is this?
   - The world's population exceeds 6 billion for the first time.
   - A total solar eclipse was visible in parts of the UK and across Europe.
   - After a gap of 16 years, a new *Star Wars* film, *Star Wars Episode I: The Phantom Menace*, is released.
   - In London, the Millennium Dome opened its doors to guests for the first time.

2. Who is this?
   - Made a Dame in the New Year's Honours of 2017 along with Patricia Routledge and Anna Wintour.
   - A stand at Sheffield United's football ground, Bramall Lane, is named after her.
   - Her time in the 100-metre hurdles, set at the London Olympics in 2012, was a new British record.
   - She was runner-up in the BBC's *Sports Personality of the Year* in 2012.

3. What is this?
   - A psychological thriller written by Patricia Highsmith about an eponymous confidence trickster.
   - Winner in 1956 of the Edgar Allan Poe Award for best novel, and later adapted for a 1999 film.
   - The protagonist commits a murder on the Italian Riviera.
   - Anthony Minghella directed the film of the novel with Matt Damon in the title role.

The answers are on page 187.

Work out the links between the answers to the questions to solve the grid. Use the grid to help you answer all the questions.

2 Across (5 letters)

1. What show, still running today, was the first programme broadcast on Channel 4 when it launched in the UK in 1982?

2. The Bolshoi Theatre in Moscow gives its name to the internationally renowned ballet that is based there. What does 'bolshoi' mean in English?

3. Who served under Tony Blair as Home Secretary from 1997 to 2001 and Foreign Secretary from 2001 to 2006?

4. Which Agatha Christie novel was subtitled 'Poirot's Last Case'?

5. What is $\frac{2}{3} \times \frac{3}{8}$?

. . . what is the link?

4 Across (6)

1. Which element is the best conductor of electricity?
2. What in mathematics is an inferential argument demonstrating that stated assumptions logically guarantee a conclusion?
3. What word goes with 'camel', 'wagon' and 'soul'?
4. What band was formed by Courtney Love in 1989?
5. In bridge, what is completed when a team win two games?

. . . what is the link?

1 Down (5)

1. What kind of tower is a magnificent-sounding place where intellectuals engage with each other detached from the real world?
2. 'Nothing left to make me feel small, luck has left me standing so tall.' What word comes next?
3. Which geological period comes after the Triassic and before the Cretaceous?
4. In basketball, what position can be 'shooting', 'point' or 'combo'?
5. Which insect kills more people than any other animal?

. . . what is the link?

3 Down (6)

1. Which London department store was founded in 1870 and is located on Great Marlborough Street?
2. What can be courtly, blind or unconditional?
3. What number can be written 1×10^3?
4. Budding flowers from what plant, *Humulus lupulus*, often seen adorning rustic country pubs, are used to give flavour and bitterness to beer?
5. Since 1301, the title of Earl of Chester has accompanied which other Royal title?

. . . what is the link?

Find the solution on page 222.

👑 FIFTY-FIFTY 3

Try to answer these fifty-fifty questions.

1. Who wrote the music, **Gilbert** or **Sullivan**?
2. What colour is the bottom stripe of the Stars and Stripes, **red** or **white**?
3. Which is larger, the **Isle of Man** or the **Isle of Wight**?
4. Which was invented first, the **zip** or **Velcro**?
5. Which entrepreneur said: 'Rockets are cool. There's no getting around that.' **Jeff Bezos** or **Elon Musk**?

Turn to page 219 for the answers.

👑 FLORA AND FAUNA

These questions are all on the topic of flora and fauna. How many can you answer?

1. How is the flower *Helianthus annuus* better known?
2. Which flower appears in the Imperial Seal of Japan?
3. What does a plant lack to be classified as herbaceous?
4. What unusual property do the *Droseraceae* family of plants have that is more normally found in animals?
5. How is the colourful, flowering house plant *Impatiens walleriana* better known?
6. A Death Cap is a poisonous what?
7. Antirrhinum is a flowering plant so named because of its resemblance to the face of a mythical creature. How is it commonly known?
8. What would a gardener use a dibber for?
9. What characteristic does a plant have in order to be classified as an angiosperm?
10. What poisonous plant means 'beautiful lady' in Italian?

The answers are on page 215.

Try to answer these miscellaneous questions:

1. Which is the most southerly racecourse in the UK?
2. Who writes crime novels under the pen name of Robert Galbraith?
3. The 'sciatic' is the largest what in the human body?
4. In *Back to the Future*, what was Doc's dog called?
5. What does 'RMS' stand for in the name of a ship (as in RMS *Titanic*)?
6. In the BBC's 'The Big Read' poll of the UK's favourite books in 2003, what was the only novel in the top 5 that was not either science fiction or fantasy?
7. The second-longest land border in the Americas, and the third-longest in the world, is between which two countries?
8. Rearranging emoticons is academic? (anag, 9)
9. What might link Joe Root, Jarvis Cocker, David Hockney and Tom Wilkinson with a Monty Python sketch?
10. What is 109m long, 73m wide and has a crew of 7 people?
11. Outkast have two members . . . André 3000 and who?
12. Which city in the UK has a local nickname of 'Auld Reekie'?
13. The German word 'brustwarzen', literally 'breast warts', translates to what word in English?
14. What type of animal were Monty, Willow and Holly, who appeared in the 2012 Olympic opening ceremony?
15. In which city can you visit Botticelli's *The Birth of Venus*?

Find the answers on page 211.

♔ CHOICE OF FOUR 4

Try to pick the correct answer for each of these questions.

1. Who is NOT a godchild of Elton John?

   A. Sean Lennon   **B.** Damian Hurley

   C. Romeo Beckham   **D.** Cara Delevingne

2. Who was the first English king after 1066 to speak English as a native language?

   A. Henry I   **B.** Henry II

   C. Henry III   **D.** Henry IV

3. What is a 'bildungsroman'?

   A. A 'whodunnit'   **B.** A coming-of-age story

   C. An epic poem   **D.** A text book

4. Which is NOT in the Arctic?

   A. Barents Sea   **B.** Beaufort Sea

   C. Bellingshausen Sea   **D.** Bering Sea

5. The young of which animal is called a 'puggle'?

   A. Pygmy hippo   **B.** Platypus

   C. Meerkat   **D.** Capybara

6. Where is the Scottish Grand National run?

   A. Ayr   **B.** Hamilton

   C. Keslo   **D.** Perth

The answers are on page 207.

THE WISDOM OF THE CROWD: BONES IN THE SPINE

The Ministry of Quizzes asked 200 people in the UK: *'How many vertebrae are there in the spine of an adult human?'* This is how they responded:

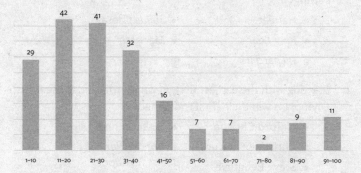

(For instance, 29 people gave an answer in the range of 1 and 10.*)

 The middle answer	26	 The most popular answer	20	 The average answer	34

21	30	25	29
The most popular answer from university-educated people	The middle answer from school-educated people	The middle answer from people aged over 30	The most popular answer for people aged 30 and under

Based on this data, or otherwise, what is *your* estimate of the number of vertebrae in the adult human spine?

The answer is on page 202.

* 4 people answered 'don't know'; their responses have not been included.

👑 PUT IN ORDER 2

Arrange the items in each of these lists in the correct order.

1. Starting with the earliest, what is the correct order of these Shakespeare plays according to the time of their historical setting?
   - *Hamlet*
   - *King Lear*
   - *Richard II*
   - *Julius Caesar*
   - *Macbeth*

2. Starting with the earliest first, in what order did these British Olympians win their (first) gold medal?
   - Linford Christie
   - Christine Ohuruogu
   - Steve Redgrave
   - Jessica Ennis-Hill
   - Ann Packer

3. Arrange these European rivers from the shortest to the longest.
   - Danube
   - Thames
   - Seine
   - Rhine
   - Shannon

4. Starting with the earliest, in what order did McDonald's establish outlets in each of these countries?
   - France
   - United Kingdom
   - Vietnam
   - Russia
   - United States

Turn to page 186 for the answers.

Try to answer these miscellaneous questions:

1. The Portuguese word for which bird means 'flower kisser'?
2. Which recording artist curates a publishing label called #Merky Books?
3. Who, through her work on Charles Babbage's Analytical Engine, is regarded as the first computer programmer?
4. What was unusual about the bat Dennis Lillee used in a test match against England in Perth in 1979?
5. The name of which iconic building in Rome means 'all gods' or 'to every god'?
6. The volume of what solid is given by the formula $\frac{4}{3}\pi r^3$?
7. What number are the clocks striking in the first line of George Orwell's *1984*?
8. What four-letter acronym, with a similar meaning to '*carpe diem*', did Drake and Lil Wayne popularize in the song 'The Motto'?
9. Which word for a legal professional comes from a medieval French word meaning 'to turn to'?
10. What links Marge Simpson and Jackie Kennedy Onassis?
11. In binary it is 1010, what is it in decimal?
12. Which is the only English county with two separate coastlines?
13. Which is the only animal in the title of a Shakespeare play?
14. How is Radio Detection and Ranging technology more commonly known?
15. Brad Pitt in 2012 was the first male ambassador of which fragrance?

Turn to page 191 for the answers.

Can you match the taglines to the films? (For a harder game, and more points, play 'blind' without the answers in the second grid.)

1.	2.	3.	4.
'Heroes aren't born, they're built'	'Think this is what they do all day?'	'May the odds be ever in your favour'	'Your mind is the scene of the crime'
5.	**6.**	**7.**	**8.**
'Help is only 140 million miles away'	'The longer you wait the harder it gets'	'Meet the little voices in your head'	'This is the story of a lifetime'
9.	**10.**	**11.**	**12.**
'We scare because we care'	'Nothing spreads like fear'	'Courage is immortal'	'All you need is one killer track'

A.	B.	C.	D.
Baby Driver	*Thor*	*The Martian*	*Inside Out*
E.	**F.**	**G.**	**H.**
The Hunger Games	*Contagion*	*The 40-Year-Old-Virgin*	*Inception*
I.	**J.**	**K.**	**L.**
Iron Man	*The Secret Life of Pets*	*Moonlight*	*Monsters, Inc.*

The solution is on page 187.

♛ COCKTAILS

How many questions on the topic of cocktails can you answer?

1. Which cocktail was invented in Raffles Hotel?
2. Which cocktail has a name that means 'strained pineapple'?
3. What '. . . and juice' is the title of a 1994 Snoop Dogg song?
4. What makes a Cosmopolitan red?
5. Which popular cocktail is served with an accompanying shot of prosecco?
6. Which cocktail means 'very good' in Tahitian?
7. What 1958 instrumental song by The Champs, named after a popular cocktail liquor, contains only three spoken words?
8. What is the main spirit in a Tom Collins?
9. Which cocktail was invented by Giuseppe Cipriani, head bartender of Harry's Bar, in Venice, in 1948?
10. Which country does a Caipirinha come from?

Go to page 198 for the answers.

♛ CONNECTIONS 3

The answers to these questions share a link . . . what is it?

1. In *The Hunger Games*, what name is given to the contestants who must fight to the death?
2. How are the Alcedinidae family of birds, noted for their bright plumage and riverside habitats, commonly known?
3. In musical notation, what 'clef' is typically found at the beginning of the lower stave of a piece of music?
4. What name is given to the male head of a monastery?
5. What is the Latin word for 'crown', used for the aura of plasma that surrounds a star?

What is the connection that the answers have in common?

Find out on page 218.

Try to pick the correct option for each of these questions.

1. Which character said: 'There are few people whom I really love, and still fewer of whom I think well'?

     A. Bridget Jones   **B.** Elizabeth Bennet

     C. Emma Woodhouse   **D.** Miss Havisham

2. Which comedy double-act once appeared in *The Sweeney*?

     A. Cannon and Ball   **B.** Little and Large

     C. Morecambe and Wise **D.** Hale and Pace

3. Where are Kalaallisut and Danish the two main languages spoken?

     A. Greenland   **B.** Iceland

     C. Norway   **D.** The Faroe Islands

4. What does the Swahili phrase '*hakuna matata*' mean in English?

     A. 'How are you doing?' **B.** 'No worries'

     C. 'See you later'   **D.** 'Take it easy'

5. What is made in the Bessemer process?

     A. Steel   **B.** Fertilizer

     C. Bread   **D.** Wine

6. Which of these cities has never hosted the Summer Olympics?

     A. Stockholm   **B.** Helsinki

     C. Amsterdam   **D.** Oslo

The answers are on page 215.

👑 IN COMMON 3

What do the terms in each of these lists have in common?

1. Philippines, Bolivia, Hungary, Kenya, Argentina.
2. Major Lazer/MØ, Luis Fonsi/Daddy Yankee, Ed Sheeran, Chance/Quavo/DJ Khaled.
3. The Moon, Phobos, Ganymede, Titan, Titania, Triton. (Be specific . . .)
4. Stephen, John, Anne, Victoria.
5. Dragon (scale), wolf (tooth), shark (maw and guff), goat (gall), tiger (chaudron).

The answers are on page 207.

👑 MOST POPULAR PUB NAMES

Try to list the **10** most popular pub names in the UK. Earn points for more obscure answers, lose points for incorrect answers.

The answers are on page 211.

👑 ODD ONE OUT 3

Which is the odd one out in each of these lists, and why?

1. Opera, Gallery, Safari, Edge, Mosaic.
2. Staten Island, Brooklyn, Queens, Harlem, The Bronx.
3. Piccolo, Oboe, Cor anglais, French horn, Bassoon.
4. Borneo, Cuba, Iceland, Madagascar, Malta.
5. Oat, Almond, Soy, Coconut, Ginger.

The answers are on page 202.

Match these song lyrics to the places in the pictures. Earn bonus points for knowing the songs and the artists.

1. This means nothing to me, Oh _____	2. Oh brother are you gonna leave me wasting away on the streets of _____	3. Baby I just wanna dance with my pretty little _____ girl
4. If you're going to _____ be sure to wear some flowers in your hair	5. _____ oriental setting and the city don't know what the city is getting	6. No sleep 'til _____
7. I met a gin-soaked bar room queen in _____	8. From Soho down to _____, I must've played 'em all	9. Flew in to _____ beach BOAC
10. Panic on the streets of London, panic on the streets of _____	11. He took me back to East Atlanta, na-na-na, oh but my heart is in _____	12. This could be Rotterdam or anywhere, _____ or Rome

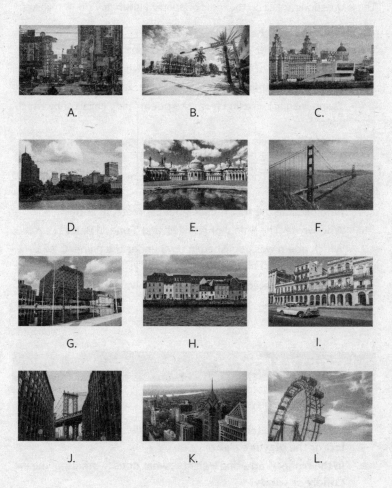

A.

B.

C.

D.

E.

F.

G.

H.

I.

J.

K.

L.

The answers are on page 198.

👑 POETRY

These questions are all on the topic of poetry. How many can you answer?

1. 'How do I love thee? Let me _____ _____ _____' what three words come next in this poem by Elizabeth Barrett Browning?
2. 'Into the valley of Death / Rode the . . .' who or what?
3. What is the first line of Sonnet 18 by Shakespeare?
4. 'Dying is an art' is a line from the poem 'Lady Lazarus' by which poet?
5. What poetic form consists of three phrases in a 5-7-5 syllable format?
6. What word in 'The Owl and the Pussy-Cat' did Edward Lear invent?
7. Who became the first female Poet Laureate, in 2009?
8. Who wrote 'The Shield of Achilles' and 'Funeral Blues'?
9. Which poem was published in 1898 under the name 'C.3.3.', standing for cell block C, landing 3, cell 3?
10. What are repeated lines in a poem, equivalent to a chorus in a song, known as?

Answers on page 194.

👑 FIFTY-FIFTY 4

Try to answer these fifty-fifty questions.

1. Which side of a tennis court is the deuce court? The **player's left** or the **player's right**?
2. In the name 'Wuthering Heights', what does 'wuthering' mean? **Lonely** or **windy**?
3. After he died, which actor was buried, at his request, in his Dracula costume? **Christopher Lee** or **Bela Lugosi**?
4. Which is the higher rank in the British navy? **Rear Admiral** or **Vice Admiral**?
5. Which is further west, **Edinburgh** or **Bristol**?

See page 191 for the answers.

Try to answer these miscellaneous questions.

1. Which Nintendo video game first featured the character of Mario?

2. Which French scientist once said 'a meal without wine is like a day without sunshine'?

3. What is the name of the fictional building in which the events of the movie *Die Hard* take place?

4. An artwork by Sarah Lucas was called *Two _____ and a Kebab*. What?

5. The Dodecanese group of islands are in which sea?

6. Whose speech, on 3 September 1939, began 'In this grave hour . . .'?

7. In a business meeting of 7 people, everybody shakes hands with each other. How many handshakes are there?

8. Who was the last British prime minister to serve two non-consecutive terms?

9. In internet slang, what does SMH stand for?

10. Which was the first Summer Olympic games that Queen Elizabeth II opened?

11. Which creature did Winnie-the-Pooh and Piglet set a trap for?

12. What does SS stand for in the name of a ship, for instance the SS *Great Britain*?

13. Where in the UK might residents affectionately be called 'Monkey hangers'?

14. Which detective dies in a story called *The Final Problem*?

15. Which is the only UK place in the title of a Shakespeare play?

Answers on page 187.

The Ministry of Quizzes translated distinctive lines from well-known karaoke classics . . . into Esperanto. Can you recognize them? (The song titles, also translated, are in brackets.)

♪ **1.**

'Du cent gradoj

Tial ili nomas min Sinjoro Fahrenheit'

('Ne Haltigu Min Nun')

♪ **2.**

'Vi devas batali! Por via rajto!

Festi!'

('Batalu Por Via Rajto (Festi)')

♪ **3.**

'Volas, ke vi sentigu min

Kiel mi estas la sola knabino en la mondo'

('Sola Knabino (en la Mondo)')

♪ **4.**

'Ho, bebo, bebo

Kiel mi supozis scii?'

('Bebo Unu Plia Tempo')

♪ **5.**

'Rigardu la hokon dum mia DJ turnas ĝin

Glacio glacio bebo'

('Glacio Glacio Bebo')

Answers on page 222.

Try to pick the correct option for each of these questions.

1. What colour is 'xanthic'?

   A. Red   **B.** Yellow

   C. Green   **D.** White

2. Which is the most expensive property on the original US Monopoly board?

   A. Pennsylvania Avenue   **B.** Boardwalk

   C. Pennsylvania Railroad   **D.** New York Avenue

3. In biology, mitochondria provide what for cells?

   A. Energy   **B.** Water

   C. Propulsion   **D.** Sensitivity

4. Which *Strictly Come Dancing* judge appeared in the video for Elton John's 'I'm Still Standing'?

   A. Shirley Ballas   **B.** Arlene Phillips

   C. Craig Revel Horwood   **D.** Bruno Tonioli

5. Which literary character said 'He's more myself than I am'?

   A. Victor Frankenstein   **B.** Catherine Earnshaw

   C. Harry Potter   **D.** Lady Macbeth

6. How was Louis XV related to Louis XIV?

   A. Nephew   **B.** Son

   C. Grandson   **D.** Great-grandson

The answers are on page 218.

Find each answer using the clues in turn – the least number of clues the better.

1. What is this?
   - It has been an Olympic athletics event since 1912.
   - As of 2021, athletes from the United States have won it 18 times to date, the most of any nation.
   - Michael Johnson won a gold medal in this event in Barcelona in 1992 but not in Atlanta in 1996 or Sydney in 2000.
   - It is the final event of the Olympic athletics programme.

2. What is this?
   - It originates in the Black Forest region of Germany, near the town of Donaueschingen.
   - It passes through a gorge called the Iron Gate, now the location of two hydroelectric dams.
   - It passes through four capital cities.
   - It inspired a waltz by Johann Strauss II.

3. Who is this?
   - He played college football for the University of Miami and entered the 1995 NFL Draft.
   - He won his first WWF Championship in 1998.
   - He is half Samoan, on his mother's side.
   - He has appeared in numerous films, including *The Scorpion King* and *Jumanji: Welcome to the Jungle*.

See page 214 for the answers.

👑 LETTER BOX 2

The clues correspond to single letters. The letters make a coiled-up, 9-letter word or name. The word can start in any square, and can run in any direction, but always through adjacent squares. Solve the clues to unscramble the word.

Clue: Before they were famous (and fabulous . . .)

Article denoting single objects	South African currency	Population growth rate
Prefix of craft commanded by Otto Kretschmer in WW2	Denoting a knight in chess	Chromosome triggering male sex development in humans
Symbol denoting quantity of electric charge	3,4-Methylene-dioxy-methamphet-amine	Had a UK hit in 1979 with 'Pop Muzik'

The answers are on page 211.

👑 CRICKET OUTS

Try to list the **10** ways of getting out in cricket. Earn points for more obscure answers, lose points for incorrect answers.

Answers on page 207.

MATCHING PAIRS: US PRESIDENTS AND EVENTS IN HISTORY

Can you match the events to the US Presidents in office at the time? (For a harder game, and more points, play 'blind' without the answers in the second grid.)

1. Louisiana Purchase	2. Shooting of Martin Luther King, Jr	3. Space Shuttle Challenger disaster	4. Attack on Pearl Harbor
5. Cuban Missile Crisis	6. Battle of Gettysburg	7. Start of Prohibition	8. Lehman's Bankruptcy
9. Moon Landings	10. Battle of the Little Bighorn	11. End of the Vietnam War	12. Start of COVID-19 pandemic

A. Ronald Reagan	B. John F. Kennedy	C. Abraham Lincoln	D. Gerald Ford
E. Lyndon B. Johnson	F. Franklin D. Roosevelt	G. Donald Trump	H. Woodrow Wilson
I. Thomas Jefferson	J. George W. Bush	K. Richard Nixon	L. Ulysses S. Grant

See page 201 for the solution.

Who or what comes next in each of these sequences?

1. Deca, Hecto, Kilo, Mega . . .?
2. Met, took for a drink, made love, made love, made love, made love . . .?
3. 1, 4, 7, 12, 16, 14 . . .?
4. Baron, Viscount, Earl, Marquess . . .?
5. Russia, Ukraine, France, Spain . . .?

The answers are on page 222.

👑 CONNECTIONS 4

The answers to these questions share a link . . . what is it?

1. What is the fruit of the *Persea americana* tree, sometimes known as an alligator pear?
2. Who was the eponymous heroine of the 1869 R. D. Blackmore novel set in Exmoor?
3. The equator passes through Brazil, Colombia and which other South American country?
4. What phrase, meaning a demanding or narcissistic person, comes from opera and the female lead, literally 'first lady'?
5. Which element is a colourless, odourless, radioactive gas, atomic number 86?

What connection do these answers share?

Find out if you are right on page 191.

Try to pick the correct option for each of these questions.

1. What does an ecdysiast do?

    A. Study wildlife   **B.** Collect fossils

    C. Take their clothes off   **D.** Perform trapeze acts

2. Which is not a dwarf in *The Hobbit*?

    A. Nori   **B.** Dori

    C. Bori   **D.** Ori

3. What is Joe Biden's home state?

    A. Delaware   **B.** Indiana

    C. Massachusetts   **D.** Vermont

4. Which European country has the lowest highest point (above sea level)?

    A. Netherlands   **B.** Malta

    C. Monaco   **D.** Vatican City

5. In *Monty Python and the Holy Grail* what question does Sir Galahad (played by Michael Palin) get wrong?

    A. 'What is your name?'   **B.** 'What is your quest?'

    C. 'What is your favourite colour?'   **D.** 'What is the airspeed velocity of an unladen swallow'?

6. Which of these chocolate bars does NOT contain nuts?

    A. Double Decker   **B.** Topic

    C. Picnic   **D.** Toblerone

The answers are on page 194.

Arrange the items in each of these lists in the correct order.

1. Starting with the smallest number first, order these national flags according to how many stars they have.
    - Australia
    - Brazil
    - Israel
    - Panama
    - United States

2. Starting with the fewest, arrange these creatures according to the number of horns they have.
    - Bull
    - Hoplitomeryx
    - Jacob sheep
    - Triceratops
    - Unicorn

3. Starting with the earliest, in what order do these sporting events occur over the calendar year?
    - Cowes Week
    - The Grand National
    - The Monaco Grand Prix
    - The Super Bowl
    - The US Open (Tennis)

4. Starting with the earliest, in what order did these events in British history take place?
    - The Battle of Blenheim
    - The Gunpowder Plot
    - The Great Fire of London
    - The birth of Shakespeare
    - Westminster Abbey consecrated

The answers are on page 185.

Try to answer these miscellaneous questions.

1. In the Marvel Cinematic Universe, the Infinity Stones are Mind, Power, Soul, Space, Time and what?

2. 'He's got morning glory and life's a different story.' What line comes next?

3. Events in which novel take place in the Overlook Hotel?

4. Ynys Môn is the Welsh name for which island?

5. What is sake brewed from?

6. What links the capital cities of Poland, Norway and Ethiopia?

7. What is Harry Potter's pet owl called?

8. In internet slang, what does BRB stand for?

9. What does Switzerland have in common with Liechtenstein, Senegal and Cameroon, and also, until 2002, had in common with France, Belgium and Luxembourg?

10. What colour are the letters G in the Google logo?

11. What type of spirit replaces vodka to turn a Bloody Mary into a Bloody Maria?

12. How is Stefani Joanne Angelina Germanotta better known?

13. As of 2021, how many British Prime Ministers were both born and served during the reign of Queen Elizabeth II?

14. Nuuk is the capital of which dependent territory?

15. 'Two fat ladies' is the bingo call for what number?

Answers on page 222.

👑 CURRY

These questions all concern Indian cuisine. How many can you answer?

1. What is the main ingredient of 'dal'?
2. What is the clarified butter used in Indian cooking called?
3. Which curry-themed song begins 'Where on earth are you from . . .'?
4. What is the characteristic ingredient of biryani?
5. What vegetable would 'gobi' be cooked with?
6. Rogan Josh is usually based on which meat?
7. What is 'murgh' on an Indian menu?
8. What dish translates as 'two onions'?
9. What are the two main ingredients of Sag Aloo?
10. Madras in India gave its name to a hot curry, what is the city now known as?

See page 218 for the answers.

👑 ODD ONE OUT 4

Which is the odd one out in each of these lists, and why?

1. Basil, Dill, Coriander, Rosemary.
2. Strait of Messina, Malacca Strait, Strait of Gibraltar, Strait of Hormuz.
3. John Adams, Benjamin Franklin, Thomas Jefferson, James Madison, James Monroe.
4. Ciambella, Fettuccine, Fusilli, Rigatoni.
5. Fermanagh, Kerry, Limerick, Tipperary.

Go to page 214 for the answers.

Work out the links between the answers to the questions to solve the grid. Use the grid to help you answer all the questions.

2 Across (7 letters)

1. Named after an English explorer, the _____ Passage is the body of water between South America and Antarctica, linking the Pacific with the Atlantic?

2. In the standard UK Monopoly, what comes immediately before each of Euston Road, Fleet Street and Park Lane?

3. Which Edgar Allan Poe story ends with the collapse of a building?

4. What three letters are the logo on the front of the time-travelling car in *Back to the Future*?

5. 'I've been cheated by you since I don't know when' . . . is the first line of which pop song?

. . . what is the link?

4 Across (6)

1. What word links a TV series starring Julianna Margulies and a TV series starring Kristen Bell?
2. Which colour absorbs the most radiation?
3. Sends word changed to go casual? (anag, 5,4)
4. Douglas is the largest place on which island?
5. Which amendment to the US Constitution abolished slavery?

. . . what is the link?

1 Down (6)

1. Which two letters link tungsten carbide and a toilet?
2. What fruit of the genus *Fragaria* is unusual in having its seeds on the outside?
3. Get manic turning into a force of attraction? (anag, 8)
4. Which Danish crime series is set in Copenhagen and features the investigations of Detective Inspector Sarah Lund?
5. In Cornwall, what type of industrial working is often prefaced with the Cornish word 'Wheal', for instance Wheal Jane, Wheal Martyn?

. . . what is the link?

3 Down (4)

1. Two lines that don't meet or intersect must be what?
2. On the London Underground map, which line is red?
3. What is the name of the ice hockey team that play at Madison Square Garden in New York?
4. What is known as 'Adam's ale' and 'the universal solvent'?
5. What Swahili word, adopted into English, means 'journey'?

. . . what is the link?

Find the solution on page 210.

✿ FIFTY-FIFTY 5

Try to answer these fifty-fifty questions.

1. Who is godmother to Brooklyn and Romeo Beckham, **Elizabeth Hurley** or **Stella McCartney**?
2. Which receives the most visitors each year, **the Eiffel Tower** or **Disneyland Paris**?
3. Which position wears number 1 in a rugby union team, **Tight Head Prop** or **Loose Head Prop**?
4. What is higher, a **Corbett** or a **Munro**?
5. Which pill does Neo take in *The Matrix*, the **red pill** or the **blue pill**?

Answers on page 207.

✿ CONNECTIONS 5

The answers to these questions share a link . . . can you work out what it is?

1. Dumbledore is an old English word for which insect?
2. What word links 'dress', 'free' and 'pants'?
3. Go variant worked out by map reader? (anag, 9)
4. What is the state capital and largest city in Arizona?
5. What tourist attraction in Rome connects the Piazza di Spagna with the Trinità dei Monti church?

What connection do these answers share?

Find out if you are right on page 201.

THE WISDOM OF THE CROWD: PROPERTIES IN MONOPOLY

The Ministry of Quizzes asked 200 people in the UK: 'How many properties are there, in total, on the Monopoly board?' This is how they responded.

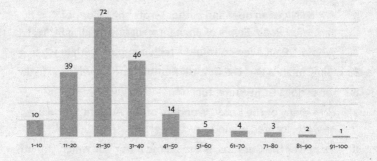

(For instance, 10 people gave an answer in the range of 1 and 10.*)

The middle answer **28**	The most popular answer **40**	The average answer **31**
26 The middle answer from people from the North	**29** The middle answer from people from the South	**25** The most popular answer from men	**29** The most popular answer from women

Based on this data, or otherwise, what is *your* estimate of the number of properties in Monopoly?

The answer is on page 198.

* 4 people answered 'don't know'; their responses have not been included.

Try to answer these miscellaneous questions.

1. Mount Narodnaya is the tallest mountain in which range?

2. What word from Latin meaning 'elsewhere' is often used in a legal context?

3. Which Nigerian poet and author wrote the trilogy of *The Famished Road*, *Songs of Enchantment* and *Infinite Riches*?

4. Who did Paul Allen co-found a tech company with in 1975?

5. 'Sing' in 2014 was the first UK number one for which artist?

6. What does GCSE stand for?

7. How many of the Seven Wonders of the Ancient World are, or were, located in modern-day Egypt?

8. 'Dance of the Cuckoos' is the theme music for which comedy double act?

9. How many piccolos of champagne would fill a magnum?

10. To the nearest 5%, how much of the Earth's surface is covered by land?

11. The four types of wetland are bog, swamp, marsh – and what?

12. Which priceless artwork that now resides in the Louvre was discovered in 1820 in a cave on the island of Milos in the Aegean?

13. What Scottish icon was named a World Heritage Site in 2015?

14. 'Satin devotee' is an anagram of the name of which burlesque model and actress?

15. Which three letters turn a verb into a gerund?

Turn to page 194 for the answers.

Try to pick the correct option for each of these questions.

1. Founded in 301 AD, what is the oldest sovereign state in Europe?

    A. San Marino   **B.** Denmark

    C. Estonia   **D.** Luxembourg

2. Which French mountain was the subject of a number of paintings by Cezanne?

    A. Mont Blanc   **B.** Mont Sainte-Victoire

    C. Mont Ventoux   **D.** Mont Aiguille

3. Mexico is crossed by . . .?

    A. The Tropic of Cancer   **B.** The Tropic of Capricorn

    C. The Equator   **D.** None of these

4. Which city did Frank Sinatra sing 'won't let you down'?

    A. New York   **B.** Chicago

    C. Los Angeles   **D.** Boston

5. Species of insects make up approximately what proportion of the world's animal species?

    A. 30%   **B.** 50%

    C. 80%   **D.** 90%

6. What year did Brazil first win the men's FIFA World Cup?

    A. 1930   **B.** 1930

    C. 1950   **D.** 1958

Find the answers on page 191.

🜲 PICTURE LOGIC: COUNTRY OUTLINES

These questions refer to the countries pictured. Some questions may give you clues to the answers to others. Use this – and your knowledge, of course – to identify as many of these countries as you can . . . then answer the questions. Note the silhouettes are all oriented with North at the top but they are not to the same scale.

1. Which *three* of these countries are in Africa?

2. Which *four* begin with the letter 'P'?

3. Which *five* end in the letter 'A'?

4. Which *five* are in the Eurozone?

5. Which *two* of these countries border each other?

6. Which has a map of itself on its flag?

7. Which *two* have borders with Russia?

8. Which *two* are landlocked?

9. Which *two* are islands?

10. Which *two* begin with the letter 'C'?

11. Which *two* are in the Southern Hemisphere?

12. Which *two* have borders with Iran?

13. Which has a compass bearing in its name?

14. Which is a member of OPEC?

15. Which *three* have flags that are red and white only?

16. Which *two* have coastlines directly on the Atlantic Ocean?

See page 186 for the solution.

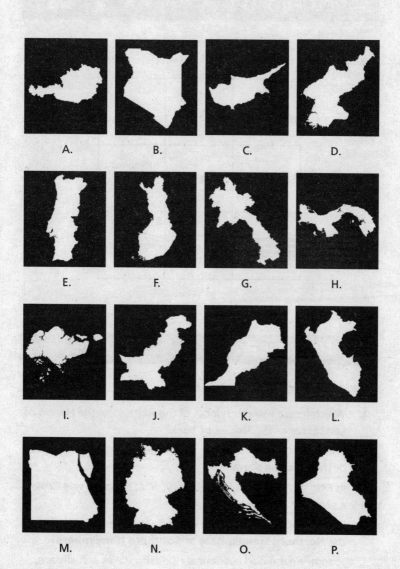

A.

B.

C.

D.

E.

F.

G.

H.

I.

J.

K.

L.

M.

N.

O.

P.

The clues in the grid relate to the numbers 1 to 9. No number is repeated. Use a process of elimination to work out which number is which.

Years duration of the American Civil War	Cat's lives	Wives of Henry VIII
Feet in a yard	Night stand	Inhabited Channel Islands
Slaughter-house	Grand-children of Elizabeth II	Atomic number of Helium

The solution is on page 222.

The solution is on page 222.

👑 FIFTY-FIFTY 6

Try to answer these fifty-fifty questions.

1. Which house had the symbol of the white rose, the **House of Lancaster** or the **House of York**?

2. From coastline to coastline, which is longer, the **Suez Canal** or the **Panama Canal**?

3. In *Finding Nemo* and *Finding Dory*, what creature was Crush, a **shark** or a **turtle**?

4. In which hemisphere of the world do cyclones spin clockwise, the **Northern Hemisphere** or **Southern Hemisphere**?

5. In 1991, what did a UK tribunal rule Jaffa Cakes actually are, **cake** or **biscuit**?

Answers on page 218.

Answers on page 218.

Find each answer using the clues in turn – the least number of clues the better.

1. Who is this?
   - She first rose to fame in the children's television series *Barney & Friends* and then in *Wizards of Waverly Place*.
   - In 2007, at the age of 17, she became what was then the youngest UNICEF ambassador.
   - On 25 September 2016 she became the first person to have 100 million followers on Instagram.
   - She has topped the Billboard Hot 100 eight times, including with 'Lose You to Love Me', 'We Don't Talk Anymore' and 'It Ain't Me'.

2. What is this?
   - It is 95% water.
   - It has three main varieties – slicing, pickling and burpless/seedless.
   - It is considered a vegetable but is botanically a fruit.
   - You could say something was 'as cool as' this.

3. What city is this?
   - It is the centre of the Klang Valley metropolitan area, one of the fastest-growing urban areas in Asia.
   - It hosted the Commonwealth Games in 1998.
   - It is located between the Titiwangsa Mountains to the east and the Strait of Malacca to the west.
   - It is home to the Petronas Towers, which were, from 1998 to 2004, the tallest buildings in the world.

Go to page 210 for the answers.

Try to answer these miscellaneous questions.

1. Which 2002 film, starring Eminem, was based on his own life story?

2. Which city is called 'Kapstadt' in its local language?

3. If you travelled in Roman Britain from Isca to Lindum via Aquae Sulis, which Roman road would you take?

4. Whose first book was titled *The Voyage of the Beagle*?

5. What is alternatively known as Sagarmatha or Chomolungma in local languages?

6. When someone says 'By Jove', who or what are they literally referring to?

7. Which computer game, designed by Alexey Pajitnov, takes its name from the Greek word for the number four?

8. Which musical, written by and originally starring Lin-Manuel Miranda, won 11 Tony Awards?

9. What is the alter ego of Steve Rogers?

10. What name is given to the fourth position in a relay race?

11. Burdock seeds were the inspiration for which modern invention?

12. Which game, developed during the Qing Dynasty, is played with 144 tiles containing pictures and Chinese symbols?

13. 'Sneakers evident' is an anagram of which literary character? (7, 8)

14. If you were watching monkeys enjoying the hot springs at Jigokudani Monkey Park, which country would you be in?

15. The probability of finding what is predicted by the Drake Equation?

Find the answers on page 214.

👑 TIME ZONES

These questions concern time zones. How many can you answer?

1. Name either of the two countries that share the border that sees the biggest change in time anywhere in the world when crossed.

2. How is Coordinated Universal Time abbreviated?

3. How many time zones does the Trans-Siberian railway span, from Moscow to Vladivostok?

4. What is the longest month in the UK?

5. If it is 12 a.m. GMT, what time is it on the International Space Station?

6. Which is the largest country to only have one time zone?

7. Which three European countries are on the same time zone as the UK?

8. What does EST stand for?

9. Benjamin Franklin is credited with proposing which system for optimising a country's useful working hours?

10. When it is 12 p.m. in Addis Ababa, what time is it in Buenos Aires? (Assuming neither country observes daylight saving time.)

The answers are on page 206.

👑 ELEMENTS WITH SYMBOLS DIFFERENT FROM THEIR NAMES

Try to list the **10** chemical elements with symbols that are different from the first two letters of their names. (For example, Helium would be a wrong answer as its symbol, He, is contained in the first two letters of its name.) Earn points for more obscure answers, lose points for incorrect answers.

Answers on page 201.

The clues in the grid correspond to numbers. The rows, columns and the two diagonals add up to the same number – the Magic Number. Use the clues to find this Magic Number and solve the grid!

Clue to the Magic Number: Hawaii.

Bottles in a Nebuchadnezzar	Countries bordering Italy	Spikes on the crown of the Statue of Liberty	Syllables in a haiku
Ladies dancing	Men on a dead man's chest	Maximum number of golf clubs a player can use in a game	Cube root of 1728
A bronze desk (anag.)	Oscars won by *Titanic*	Limbs on a crab (including claws)	Age in the UK at which you can buy aerosol paint
Furlongs in a mile	Minimum age to be UK Prime Minister	Adele's first album	Years reign of Mary I of England

See page 197 for the solution.

👑 MORE, LESS OR THE SAME? 2

Which of these is more, which is less . . . or are they the same?

1. Which are there more of, years since the **fall of the Berlin Wall**, or years since **Nelson Mandela was released from prison**? Or are they the same?

2. Which number is larger, **27^2** or **9^3**? Or are they the same?

3. Who wrote the most novels, **Charles Dickens** or **Thomas Hardy**? Or were they the same?

4. Which are there more of at the start of a game, **chess pieces** or **backgammon counters**? Or are they the same?

5. What are there more of – floors in **the Shard,** in London, or floors in **the Chrysler Building**, in New York? Or are they the same?

Answers on page 194.

👑 CONNECTIONS 6

The answers to these questions share a link . . . what is it?

1. What phase of software development is given over to checking and removing bugs after the main features have been set?

2. Where in the Northeast of England would you find the Millennium Bridge and the Baltic Centre for Contemporary Art?

3. What was Muhammad Ali's self-appointed nickname?

4. The musical *Starlight Express* was notable for which type of footwear worn by the performers?

5. 'Pacific', 'Eurasian', 'Indo-Australian' and 'Nazca' are examples of which geological feature?

What connection do these answers share?

Find out if you are right on page 194.

Try to pick the correct option for each of these questions.

1. What is a funambulist?
   - **A.** A cocktail maker
   - **B.** A wind tunnel
   - **C.** A shell collector
   - **D.** A tightrope walker

2. Which is not a dimension of *Minecraft*?
   - **A.** The Overworld
   - **B.** The Underworld
   - **C.** The Nether
   - **D.** The End

3. On average, which of these is the world's longest species of snake?
   - **A.** Green Anaconda
   - **B.** Yellow Anaconda
   - **C.** Burmese Python
   - **D.** Reticulated Python

4. Croesus, King of Lydia, was the first to mint gold coins. In which modern-day country is Lydia?
   - **A.** Turkey
   - **B.** Syria
   - **C.** Iran
   - **D.** Iraq

5. Who was the last 'owner' of the Elder Wand before Harry Potter?
   - **A.** Voldemort
   - **B.** Snape
   - **C.** Dumbledore
   - **D.** Draco Malfoy

6. What was the first National Park in the UK?
   - **A.** Lake District
   - **B.** Peak District
   - **C.** Snowdonia
   - **D.** Dartmoor

The answers are on page 186.

👑 IN COMMON 4

What do the terms in each of these lists have in common?

1. Old, rusty, salty, dirty, bloody.
2. Emperor Qin, King Philip II of Spain, Mohammed bin Saud, Christopher Columbus, Simón Bolívar.
3. Savile, Brick, Abbey, King's, Baker.
4. Pablo Picasso 1967, Jasper Johns 1988, Damien Hirst 2007, Jeff Koons 2013, David Hockney 2018.
5. Counter, sofa, shower, on camera.

Go to page 221 for the answers.

👑 AIRPORTS

These questions all concern airports. How many can you answer?

1. Which airport has a name which means 'Goat Farm' in Old English?
2. If you were travelling to an airport with the IATA code ORY, which country would you be visiting?
3. PSY is the IATA code for which remote island airport?
4. Which city is served by Haneda and Narita airports?
5. What is the main airport serving Chicago?
6. Which airport has the IATA code DXB?
7. Which US airport is a Sky Harbor?
8. Washington, D.C.'s airport is named after which US President?
9. An airport in which European country is named after Mother Teresa?
10. The route between which two international airports earns the most revenue for the airlines that operate it?

Go to page 218 for the answers.

Try to answer these miscellaneous questions.

1. The A282 links the north and south ends of which motorway?
2. The ban on which book was lifted in the UK in 1960?
3. What does Mardi Gras mean in English?
4. Which David Bowie song has been covered by Lulu and Nirvana?
5. What was constructed in August 1961 and demolished in November 1989?
6. Which is the most southerly city in the UK?
7. *Citrus sinensis* is the Latin name for which fruit?
8. The largest football stadium in the world has a capacity of 114,000 people. What country is it in?
9. Which writer created Humpty Dumpty?
10. What colour is verdigris?
11. 'Poke my nuzzle' is an anagram of which tree?
12. Which outlaw died at the age of 21, killed by Sheriff Pat Garrett?
13. If you ordered '*cuisses de grenouille*' what would you be eating?
14. The climax to which 1989 action film was filmed in the ancient city of Petra?
15. Wallonia is a French-speaking region of which country?

Go to page 210 for the answers.

THE WISDOM OF THE CROWD: SHAKESPEARE PLAYS

The Ministry of Quizzes asked 200 people in the UK: '*How many plays did William Shakespeare write?*' This is how they responded:

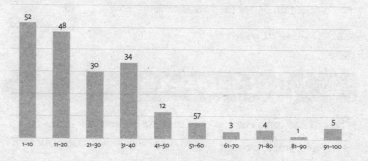

(For instance, 52 people gave an answer in the range of 1 and 10.*)

The middle answer **20**	The most popular answer **20**	The average answer **26**
25 The middle answer from university-educated people	**20** The middle answer from school-educated people	**20** The most popular answer from men

| **37** The most popular answer from women |

Based on this data, or otherwise, what is *your* estimate of the number of plays written by Shakespeare?

The answer is on page 214.

* 4 people answered 'don't know'; their responses have not been included.

👑 LOSING FIFA WORLD CUP NATIONS

Try to list the **10** nations that have been a losing finalist at least once in a FIFA World Cup final (as of 2021). Earn points for more obscure answers, lose points for incorrect answers. (Note that this applies to the men's competition, and that some on this list may have also won the competition on another occasion.)

Go to page 206 for the answers.

👑 WHAT COMES NEXT? 4

Who or what comes next in each of these sequences?

1. Face, grace, woe, go . . .?
2. Christie, Bailey, Greene, Gatlin . . .?
3. Sedgefield, Dunfermline East, Witney, Maidenhead . . .?
4. CR, QOS, S, S . . .?
5. Jane, Elizabeth, Mary, Kitty . . .?

Go to page 201 for the answers.

👑 IN COMMON 5

What do the terms in each of these lists have in common?

1. The Oval, Crystal Palace, Bramall Lane, Wembley Stadium, the Principality Stadium.
2. Sucre, Togrog, Colon, Lek, Won.
3. Florence Nightingale, Charles Dickens, Charles Darwin, Jane Austen.
4. Netherlands, Gambia, Bahamas, Philippines.
5. White, Boots, Forty, Goose, Wood.

Find the answers on page 197.

Try to pick the correct option for each of these questions.

1. What river is York on?
   - **A.** Ribble
   - **B.** Derwent
   - **C.** Ouse
   - **D.** Trent

2. *Breaking Dawn* is the last novel in which series of books?
   - **A.** *Percy Jackson and the Olympians*
   - **B.** *Vampire Academy*
   - **C.** *The Infernal Devices*
   - **D.** *Twilight*

3. The Egyptians believed the weight of which body part determined whether on your death you would be allowed into the afterlife?
   - **A.** Liver
   - **B.** Heart
   - **C.** Spleen
   - **D.** Appendix

4. 'So you can keep me inside the pocket of your ripped jeans.' Who sang these words?
   - **A.** Ed Sheeran
   - **B.** Meghan Trainor
   - **C.** Lewis Capaldi
   - **D.** James Blunt

5. Approximately how many times does a human heart beat in a day?
   - **A.** 1,000
   - **B.** 10,000
   - **C.** 100,000
   - **D.** 1,000,000

6. Which suburb of the Italian city of Trieste gives its name to a sparkling wine?
   - **A.** Freixenet
   - **B.** Asti Spumanti
   - **C.** Vida Bonita
   - **D.** Prosecco

See page 194 for the answers.

👑 FORMERLY KNOWN AS . . .

These questions are about things that were originally called something else. How many can you answer?

1. What TV quiz was originally called *Cash Mountain*?
2. Which tube line was originally going to be called the Viking Line?
3. What was originally named *Murder at Tudor Close*?
4. Which European capital city was formerly known as Christiana?
5. What book was originally titled *Tomorrow is Another Day*?
6. What did New York's Longacre Square become when it changed its name in 1904?
7. Which religious building, originally called Cappella Magna, takes its name from Pope Sixtus IV who restored it in 1480?
8. Which UK city was once known as Monkchester?
9. What modern country used to be called the Trucial States?
10. What classic novel was originally titled *First Impressions*?

See page 190 for the answers.

👑 SMALL COUNTRIES

Try to list the **10** smallest sovereign countries by area. (If it helps, Grenada is eleventh on the list with an area of 344 km² – these are all smaller than that.) Earn points for more obscure answers, lose points for incorrect answers.

The answers are on page 186.

Arrange the items in each of these lists in the correct order.

1. Starting with the fewest, what is the correct order for these sporting achievements?

   - Tom Brady Super Bowl wins
   - Serena Williams Grand Slam singles titles
   - Jack Nicklaus golf Majors
   - Pelé FIFA World Cup wins
   - Sebastian Vettel Formula 1 championships

2. Starting with the fewest, order these fantasy series according to the number of books they have.

   - *The Chronicles of Narnia*
   - *His Dark Materials*
   - *Percy Jackson and the Olympians*
   - *Discworld*
   - *Twilight*

3. Put these lines from Abba's 'Dancing Queen' in the order they are first heard in the song.

   - 'And when you get the chance'
   - 'Friday night and the lights are low'
   - 'Young and sweet only seventeen'
   - 'Feel the beat from the tambourine'
   - 'Night is young and the music's high'

4. Starting with the earliest, put these leaders of the Soviet Union in chronological order.

   - Yuri Andropov
   - Mikhail Gorbachev
   - Joseph Stalin
   - Leonid Brezhnev
   - Nikita Khrushchev

Go to page 205 for the answers.

👑 WHAT COMES NEXT? 5

Who or what comes next in each of these sequences?

1. Sea, lullabies, alibis, pay, me, eyes . . .?
2. May, July, March, August, October, February . . .?
3. Baker Street, Great Portland Street, Euston Square . . .?
4. Captain, Major, Lieutenant-Colonel, Colonel . . .?
5. Hydrogen, Helium, Lithium, Beryllium, Boron . . .?

Find the answers on page 214.

👑 ODD ONE OUT 5

Which is the odd one out in each of these lists, and why?

1. Astatine, Benzidine, Chlorine, Iodine.
2. Dua Lipa, Lady Gaga, Lorde, Pink.
3. James I, Charles II, Anne, George I.
4. *The Enormous Crocodile, Esio Trot, Mister Magnolia, The Twits.*
5. Basketball, Beach Volleyball, Cricket, Hockey.

Find the answers on page 218.

👑 SHAKESPEARE TRAGEDIES

Try to list the **10** Shakespeare plays that are normally regarded as tragedies. Earn points for more obscure answers, lose points for incorrect answers.

See page 210 for the answers.

Try to pick the correct option for each of these questions.

1. The conflict between Britain and Spain from 1739 to 1748 was known as the 'War of Jenkins' __'. What?

   A. Ear   **B.** Nose

   C. Chin   **D.** Wife

2. What does 'kraftwerk' mean in German?

   A. Factory   **B.** Power station

   C. Pottery   **D.** Manufacturing

3. On which New York Avenue is the Empire State Building?

   A. Madison Avenue   **B.** Fifth Avenue

   C. Sixth Avenue   **D.** Seventh Avenue

4. *Confessions on a Dance Floor* is an album by who?

   A. Kylie Minogue   **B.** Sophie Ellis-Bextor

   C. Madonna   **D.** Donna Summer

5. In the novel series, Percy Jackson first meets his friend Annabeth Chase after defeating what monster?

   A. Minotaur   **B.** Manticore

   C. Medusa   **D.** Hydra

6. How many cubic centimetres are there in a cubic metre?

   A. 100   **B.** 10,000

   C. 100,000   **D.** 1,000,000

The answers are on page 206.

Can you match the pairs of words to make phrases of a nautical origin? (For a harder game, and more points, play 'blind' without the answers in the second grid.)

1. Cat	2. Pipe	3. Over	4. Foot
5. Cut	6. Hard	7. Loose	8. True
9. By	10. Batten	11. Touch	12. Hand

A. Loose	B. Fast	C. Large	D. Go
E. Down	F. Fist	G. Jib	H. Barrel
I. Cannon	J. Colours	K. Bag	L. Hatches

Go to page 197 for the solution.

The answers to these questions share a link . . . what is it?

1. Got saffron cooked for this dish? (anag, 10)
2. What word goes with 'coffee', 'control' and 'zero'?
3. Who had a horse called Copenhagen?
4. What common salad ingredient, *Solanum lycopersicum*, did the US Supreme Court declare, in 1893, was a vegetable?
5. Which NBA star and member of the LA Lakers was killed in a helicopter crash in 2020?

What connection do these answers share?

Find out if you are right on page 190.

👑 THE SOVIET UNION

These questions concern the Soviet Union. How many can you answer?

1. What was Petrograd renamed when the Soviet Union was founded?
2. Who was the last leader of the Soviet Union?
3. The flag of the USSR featured a hammer, sickle and which other symbol?
4. The Molotov–Ribbentrop non-aggression pact was signed between the Soviet Union and which other country?
5. What according to Winston Churchill ran from Stettin in the Baltic to Trieste in the Adriatic?
6. A 1975 mutiny aboard the Soviet navy frigate *Storozhevoy* became the basis for which Tom Clancy story?
7. Of which former Soviet state is Yerevan the capital?
8. What does SALT stand for?
9. Which European country did the Soviet Union invade in the spring of 1968?
10. 'Moscow girls make me sing and shout' is a lyric from which song?

Turn to page 218 for the answers.

Try to answer these miscellaneous questions.

1. Who was previously the last to do what Tiger Roll did in 2019?
2. Which superhero shares their name with a town in Turkey?
3. What word, meaning the part of a loom that goes back and forth, has given us a word for transport that does something similar?
4. Which place in the UK has the post code 'EH'?
5. On which day of the week did Christopher Columbus discover Dominica?
6. In *Twilight*, what causes Bella to faint in her science class?
7. What fruit has a variety called a donut?
8. What might have just happened to make a German say 'Gesundheit'?
9. Constructed in 2630 BC, what was King Djoser the first person to build?
10. Of what sport is the WT the governing federation?
11. Entangle apt to disentangle this dynasty? (anag, 11)
12. Which sci-fi movie features a spaceship called *The Nostromo*?
13. *Ursus maritimus* is the Latin name for which animal?
14. Which year followed 1 BC?
15. What turns a croque monsieur into a croque madame?

Answers on page 190.

♔ THE WISDOM OF THE CROWD: VICTORIA'S REIGN

The Ministry of Quizzes asked 200 people in the UK: '*How long in years was the reign of Queen Victoria?*' This is how they responded:

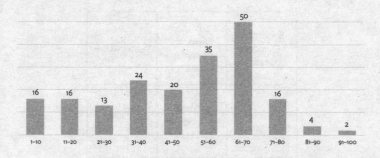

(For instance, 16 people gave an answer in the range of 1 and 10.*)

The middle answer **57**	The most popular answer **60**	The average answer **49**
60	**50**	**60**	**52**
The middle answer from men	The middle answer from women	The most popular answer from people from the North	The most popular answer from people from the South

Based on this data, or otherwise, what is *your* estimate of the length of the reign of Victoria?

The answer is on page 186.

* 4 people answered 'don't know'; their responses have not been included.

The clues in the grid relate to the numbers 1 to 9. No number is repeated. Use a process of elimination to work out which number is which.

Seekers in a Quidditch team	Summer Olympics hosted in the US	Years in Tibet
Planets in the Solar System	Segments in a standard Yorkie bar	Smallest prime number
Snow White's dwarfs with beards	Red Arrow aircraft in an air display team	Letters in the shortest name of an element

Solution on page 221.

👑 FIFTY-FIFTY 7

Try to answer these fifty-fifty questions.

1. What is a resident of Sydney known as, a '**Sydneyonian**' or a '**Sydneysider**'?

2. Who had the greater income, **Mr Darcy** or **Mr Bingley**?

3. Which opened first, the **Forth Bridge** or **Tower Bridge**?

4. Where are the Taurus Mountains, **Morocco** or **Turkey**?

5. Which cartoon character was 'a gentleman, a scholar and an acrobat', **Top Cat** or the **Pink Panther**?

Find the answers on page 201.

👑 ODD ONE OUT 6

Which is the odd one out in each of these lists, and why?

1. Chemistry, Economics, Geography, Literature, Physics.
2. Vienna, Bratislava, Budapest, Belgrade, Bucharest.
3. 1, 5, 10, 20, 50, 100.
4. Abraham Lincoln, James Garfield, Franklin D. Roosevelt, John F. Kennedy, Richard Nixon.
5. Monk, Friar, Parson, Bishop, Wife of Bath.

See page 214 for the answers.

👑 CITIES

These questions are all about cities. How many can you answer?

1. In an alphabetical list of world capital cities, which is last?
2. What was Danzig renamed in 1945?
3. What was the first city in the Southern Hemisphere to host the Olympics?
4. Which Scottish city was formerly called St Johnstone, a name retained by its football team?
5. Islamabad was built to replace which city as Pakistan's capital?
6. *A Room with a View* by E. M. Forster is largely set in which Italian city?
7. What Japanese city in Aichi Prefecture shares its name with the car manufacturer that is headquartered there?
8. What was the first city to host the World Cup final for a second time?
9. As of 2021, in which city is Europe's tallest building?
10. 'Rotten tokens' is an anagram of which UK city?

Go to page 209 for the answers.

👑 PICTURE LOGIC: BRITISH AND ENGLISH MONARCHS

These questions refer to the British and English monarchs pictured. Some questions may give you clues to the answers to others. Use this – and your knowledge, of course – to identify as many of these monarchs as you can . . . and answer the questions. All these monarchs reigned post 1066.

1. Which *seven* are Plantagenets? (Assume the Plantagenet line ran from 1154–1485)

2. Which *three* are called Henry?

3. Which *two* were married to each other?

4. Which *two* are from the House of Lancaster?

5. Which *two* are called George?

6. Which *three* are called Richard?

7. What is the sum of the regnal numbers of the monarchs on the top row?

8. Which was the first to visit China?

9. Which *four* are siblings? (2 sets)

10. Which *two* preceded and succeeded each other?

11. Which *three* have ruled for more than 50 years?

12. Which *two* went mad?

13. Which *three* do not have regnal numbers, because their names are (so far) unique in the monarchy?

14. Which *two* were from the House of Hanover? (Assume the Hanover line ran from 1714–1901)

15. Which signed the Magna Carta?

16. Which *three* have a regnal number of III?

Go to page 206 for the solution.

A.

B.

C.

D.

E.

F.

G.

H.

I.

J.

K.

L.

M.

N.

O.

P.

Try to answer these miscellaneous questions.

1. What is the name of the bioengineered androids in *Blade Runner*?

2. Whose 2018 autobiography is titled *Becoming*?

3. In biology, what can be grouped as long, short, flat, sesamoid or irregular?

4. Which sporting event was moved for three years during World War I to be held at Gatwick, on the site now occupied by the airport?

5. '. . . whence all but he had fled/The flame that lit the battle's wreck/Shone round him o'er the dead' . . . What is the first line of this poem?

6. What links Tommy Cooper, Eric Morecambe and Steve Irwin?

7. He's a speaker rewritten by this wordsmith? (anag, 11)

8. What are musophobics afraid of?

9. In 2003 the BBC ran a 'Big Read' poll to find the UK's favourite books. What was the only novel in the top 10 by a non-British author?

10. What relationship is shared between both the 2nd and 6th US Presidents, and the 41st and 43rd?

11. What fairy tale is called 'Rotkäppchen' in German and 'Roodkapje' in Dutch?

12. What protection for authors became law in 1709?

13. What is 20 metres tall and has a wingspan of 54 metres?

14. Which sports team is supported by fans known as the Tifosi?

15. Continental ops rebuilt this historic city? (anag, 14)

Answers on page 200.

FIFTY-FIFTY 8

Try to answer these fifty-fifty questions.

1. In what direction (when looked at from below) does a honey-suckle twine its stem as it climbs, **clockwise** or **anti-clockwise**?
2. What animal appears in the Slazenger logo, **Panther** or **Puma**?
3. How is Peter Parker's alter ego written, **Spider-Man** or **Spiderman**?
4. From which side of the stage does the pantomime villain traditionally enter, **stage right** or **stage left**? (As the actor faces the audience.)
5. Where was Napoleon exiled after the Battle of Waterloo, **Saint Helena** or **Elba**?

Answers on page 197.

DETECTIVES

These questions concern detectives. How many can you answer?

1. Which well-known detective retired to keep bees?
2. Who had a UK hit in 1983 with 'We are Detective'?
3. *The Killing, The Bridge* and *Bordertown* are examples of what genre of crime fiction?
4. Which TV detective had a basset hound called 'Dog'?
5. Captain Harold C. Dobey was the boss of which pair of police detectives?
6. Who played Chief Inspector John Luther?
7. DI Alec Hardy and DS Ellie Miller investigate murders in a TV series set in which county of the UK?
8. Which detective was introduced in a novel called *Murder at the Vicarage*?
9. In which 1974 film did Jack Nicholson win an Oscar for playing a private detective?
10. Who played Inspector Jane Tennison?

The answers are on page 193.

Arrange the items in each of these lists in the correct order.

1. Starting with the earliest first, what is the correct order of these Bond Girls in order of when they appeared in the film series?

    - Pam Bouvier
    - Pussy Galore
    - Tiffany Case
    - Xenia Onatopp
    - Melina Havelock

2. Starting with the smallest, put these celestial objects in order of size.

    - Betelgeuse
    - The Crab Nebula
    - Ganymede
    - Pluto
    - The Sun

3. From the lowest to the highest value, what is the correct order of these poker hands?

    - 'Broadway'
    - 'Four Horsemen'
    - 'Golf Bag'
    - 'Huey, Dewey and Louie'
    - 'Snake Eyes'

4. Starting with the smallest first, put these countries in order of size by area.

    - Iceland
    - Ivory Coast
    - Jamaica
    - Mexico
    - Turkey

Find the answers on page 220.

Find each answer using the clues in turn – the least number of clues the better.

1. What is this?
   - Prior to its release in April 2013, it had taken approximately 18 months to produce.
   - It was the most streamed song in the UK in 2013.
   - Pharrell Williams and Nile Rodgers collaborated on the song.
   - It contains the line 'She's up all night 'til the sun, I'm up all night to get some.'

2. When (which year) is this?
   - The Space Shuttle Atlantis completes STS-135, the final mission of the Space Shuttle programme.
   - Osama bin Laden is killed by a US military operation in Pakistan.
   - A 9.0 magnitude earthquake hits the east coast of Japan, and subsequent tsunamis cause widespread devastation, including to the Fukushima nuclear power station.
   - Prince William and Kate Middleton marry in Westminster Abbey in London, watched by a global audience of 2 billion people.

3. Who is this?
   - In Shakespeare, this eponymous character says: 'O no, alas, I rather hate myself/For hateful deeds committed by myself. I am a villain.'
   - He was named Lord Protector of England in 1483 on the death of Edward IV.
   - His death ended the Plantagenet line of English monarchs.
   - The whereabouts of his resting place was unknown until 2017, when remains found under a Leicester car park were identified through DNA testing.

Turn to page 190 for the answers.

Try to pick the correct option for each of these questions.

1. 'How sharper than a serpent's tooth it is to have a thankless child.' Which play does this line come from?

    A. *Henry V*   **B.** *King Lear*

    C. *Macbeth*   **D.** *Romeo and Juliet*

2. What happens if a luchador – a Mexican wrestler – removes another's mask during a fight?

    A. He must take off his own mask   **B.** He must wear it from now on

    C. He is disqualified   **D.** He wins the fight

3. The Battle of the Coral Sea was fought between Japan, the US and which other nation?

    A. Australia   **B.** Britain

    C. China   **D.** France

4. Where is Beachy Head?

    A. Cornwall   **B.** Dorset

    C. East Sussex   **D.** Kent

5. 'Moon-shot, Woodstock, Watergate . . .' What comes next, in Billy Joel's 'We Didn't Start the Fire'?

    A. 'Mr Spock'   **B.** 'Gridlock'

    C. 'Punk Rock'   **D.** 'Hitchcock'

6. In which household appliance would you find a magnetron?

    A. Fridge   **B.** Microwave oven

    C. Washing machine   **D.** Vacuum cleaner

Go to page 221 for the answers.

The clues in the grid correspond to numbers. The rows, columns and the two diagonals add up to the same number – the Magic Number. Use the clues to find this Magic Number and solve the grid!

Clue to the Magic Number: The number of tiles in a standard domino set.

Stripes on the Stars and Stripes	Nickels in a dime	IX	Noble Truths (in Buddhism)
Stars in a binary system	Pipers piping	3!	Al Pacino Oscar nominations
Marx Brothers	Gallon hat	Paintings sold by Vincent van Gogh in his lifetime	Labours of Hercules
UK number ones by the Rolling Stones	Minimum moves needed by a pawn to become a queen	Sides on a £1 coin	*Lions on a Shirt*

Turn to page 217 for the solution.

Try to answer these miscellaneous questions.

1. Museum disguised in hat regime? (anag, 9)
2. What does DVLA stand for?
3. What flavour of Walkers Crisps comes in a lime-green-coloured bag?
4. Which is the first of the Five Stages of Grief?
5. Which team have held the FA Cup for the longest period, 7 years?
6. The last words of George V were reputedly 'Bugger . . .' Which English town?
7. In which country is Timbuktu?
8. Which Ethiopian athlete set 27 world records between 1994 and 2009?
9. In the Thomas Hardy novel, at which now popular tourist attraction is Tess Durbeyfield arrested for murder?
10. What prestigious title does Sulley (the furry blue ogre) hold at the beginning of *Monsters, Inc.*?
11. In *Game of Thrones*, which city is the seat of the Iron Throne?
12. Which scientist did artists Jake and Dinos Chapman put at the peak of their rocky installation, *Ubermensch*?
13. What animal is known collectively as a tuxedo?
14. How is an 'Aktiebolaget Svenska Gasaccumulator' more commonly known?
15. Who was Roman emperor during the uprising of the Iceni in AD 60, led by Boudicca?

The answers are on page 213.

The clues correspond to single letters. The letters make a coiled-up, 9-letter word. The word can start in any square, and can run in any direction, but always through adjacent squares. Solve the clues to unscramble the word.

Clue: A country

Top of a compass	Nickname of Melbourne Cricket Ground	Retinol vitamin
Square root of -1	$= mc^2$	Music direction to play softly
SI unit for time	Played by John Cleese in *The World Is Not Enough*	Blood type of a universal donor

The answers are on page 217.

What do the terms in each of these lists have in common?

1. Reece, pain, man, inland, ran.
2. Robbie Savage, Gary Neville, Howard Wilkinson, Mark Lawrenson, Jason McAteer.
3. Top, every man, drag, prawn, Ventura.
4. Peter, Benjamin, Jeremy, Tom, Jemima.
5. Suez, Panama City, Istanbul, Magnitogorsk.

See page 201 for the answers.

Try to pick the correct option for each of these questions.

1. Spermaphobia is the fear of what?
   - **A.** Sex
   - **B.** Germs
   - **C.** Pollen
   - **D.** Gases

2. Which Mexican dish means 'little donkey'?
   - **A.** Burrito
   - **B.** Enchilada
   - **C.** Chimichanga
   - **D.** Fajita

3. A molecule of which of these does not contain a hydrogen atom?
   - **A.** Sugar
   - **B.** Salt
   - **C.** Vinegar
   - **D.** Water

4. It sold at auction in 2017 for $450 million, making 'Salvator Mundi' the world's most expensive painting. Who painted it?
   - **A.** Leonardo da Vinci
   - **B.** Botticelli
   - **C.** Pablo Picasso
   - **D.** Raphael

5. Which battle, that changed the course of English history, was fought on Senlac Hill?
   - **A.** Hastings
   - **B.** Naseby
   - **C.** Bosworth Field
   - **D.** Edington

6. Kampala is the capital of which country?
   - **A.** Pakistan
   - **B.** Burundi
   - **C.** Somalia
   - **D.** Uganda

Find the answers on page 205.

Arrange the items in each of these lists in the correct order.

1. Starting with the smallest, put these balls in order of size.

   - Hockey ball
   - Polo ball
   - Snooker ball
   - Softball
   - Tennis ball

2. Starting with the earliest, in what order did these historical events take place?

   - Abolition of slavery in the US
   - Habeas Corpus Act passed
   - Universal declaration of human rights
   - Signing of the Magna Carta
   - 'I have a dream' speech

3. Starting with the cheapest, put these movies in order of size of their budget.

   - *Avengers: Endgame*
   - *Who Framed Roger Rabbit*
   - *Spectre*
   - *Titanic*
   - *Harry Potter and the Half-Blood Prince*

4. From the shortest to the tallest, arrange these trees in order of height.

   - Coast Redwood
   - Douglas Fir
   - Dwarf Willow
   - Oak
   - Olive

The answers are on page 199.

👑 LINKOPHILIA 3

Work out the links between the answers to the questions to solve the grid. Use the grid to help you answer all the questions.

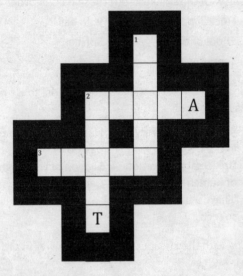

2 Across (5 letters)

1. What type of fish can be electric, shovelnose, eagle and manta?

2. In volleyball, which defensive position plays close to the net, often jumping high to block shots and deflect the ball back into the opponents' court?

3. Mice run at sixes and sevens? (anag, 7)

4. What word goes with 'side', 'safe' and 'best'?

5. Leptons, quarks and gauge bosons are elementary what?

. . . what is the link?

3 Across (5)

1. The 630-foot monument in St Louis, Missouri, is the world's tallest example of what type of structure?
2. What does the 'p' of plc stand for?
3. What 2013 song was a hit for Robin Thicke and Pharrell Williams?
4. What links 'reason', 'reach' and 'an inch'?
5. What word, used of living beings, means susceptible to death?

. . . what is the link?

1 Down (5)

1. In biology and the taxonomy of living things, what order of classification is above genus and below order?
2. Clough, glen, combe and dale are alternative words for which landscape feature?
3. What festival was banned in England from 1647 until 1660?
4. What word can mean any material substance through which waves or energy can propagate, and someone who communes with spirits?
5. Which character did Roger Lloyd-Pack portray in *Only Fools and Horses*?

. . . what is the link?

2 Down (5)

1. Americans call it a station wagon, what is it called in the UK?
2. What biological structure is a fibre or bundle of fibres that transmits impulses of sensation?
3. What is the defining characteristic of Open Source software?
4. What is a snooker shot where a player attempts to pot or hit a ball indirectly via a cushion?
5. In art, what is the complementary colour to blue?

. . . what is the link?

Find the solution on page 193.

Try to pick the correct option for each of these questions.

1. Which hospital department would you visit with a broken leg?

    A. Orthopaedics   **B.** Ophthalmology

    C. Obstetrics   **D.** Oncology

2. What is the sum of the titles of Adele's first three albums?

    A. 45   **B.** 47

    C. 65   **D.** 67

3. Who is the only player to have scored in the FIFA World Cup finals in his teens, twenties and thirties?

    A. Lionel Messi   **B.** Pelé

    C. Lothar Matthäus   **D.** Cristiano Ronaldo

4. Sir Antony Gormley's *Another Place*, an installation of 100 cast-iron figures facing out to sea, is located where in the UK?

    A. Crosby Beach in Merseyside   **B.** Morecambe Bay in Lancashire

    C. Holkham Beach in Norfolk   **D.** Seascale in Cumbria

5. In which region of Spain is the town of Guernica, which suffered bombing by Nazi planes and is the subject of the famous painting by Picasso?

    A. Andalusia   **B.** Basque Country

    C. Catalonia   **D.** Galicia

6. Podgorica is the capital of which country?

    A. Belarus   **B.** Bosnia and Herzegovina

    C. Montenegro   **D.** Tajikistan

The answers are on page 190.

Try to answer these miscellaneous questions.

1. In darts, what score is known as a 'basement'?

2. What is the longest river in the British Isles?

3. Which type of plant is studied by a pteridologist?

4. What name links *James and the Giant Peach* and *Only Fools and Horses*?

5. Only two species of mammal lay eggs, echidna is one, what is the other?

6. What mathematical proposition conjectured in 1637 was finally proven in 1995?

7. In which sport do teams compete for the Bledisloe Cup?

8. Romantics rearranging snail event? (anag, 10)

9. In which 1978 film do Susannah York and Marlon Brando play doomed parents, forced to send their baby child away?

10. Which map is the basis for Simon Patterson's work, *The Great Bear*?

11. What does the 'U' stand for in U-boat?

12. In which US state is Gettysburg?

13. Which prolific romantic novelist was also an early gliding enthusiast, who pioneered the aircraft-towed glider?

14. Who is the first character to join Dorothy on the Yellow Brick Road?

15. Which city in Scotland shares its postcode with a blood group?

Go to page 221 for the answers.

Find each answer using the clues in turn – the least number of clues the better.

1. What is this?
   - Its name is a Celtic word meaning 'border'.
   - It rises in the Lowther Hills and flows for 97 miles via Melrose, Kelso and Coldstream into the North Sea.
   - It has given its name to a type of cloth.
   - It forms the historic border between England and Scotland.

2. Who is this?
   - He died at the Hotel d'Alsace in Paris at the age of 46.
   - He sued John Douglas, the 9th Marquess of Queensberry, for criminal libel, an action which ultimately led to his own prosecution and imprisonment.
   - He once said, 'I can resist anything but temptation.'
   - He wrote the plays *Lady Windermere's Fan*, *A Woman of No Importance* and *An Ideal Husband*.

3. When (which year) is this?
   - The FA Premier League is launched in England.
   - A fire breaks out at Windsor Castle, causing the Queen to later describe the year as her 'annus horribilis'.
   - Bill Clinton is elected as the 42nd President of the United States.
   - A unified Germany competes at the Olympics for the first time, and states of the former Soviet Union compete as the 'Unified Team'.

Answers on page 185.

Try to answer these fifty-fifty questions.

1. In which state is the Statue of Liberty, **New York** or **New Jersey**?
2. In Tinder, which way do you swipe to 'like' someone, **right** or **left**?
3. Which are there more of, **trees on Earth** or **stars in our galaxy**?
4. In boxing, which is the heavier, **Featherweight** or **Bantamweight**?
5. Xanthophobia is the fear of which colour, **black** or **yellow**?

See page 213 for the answers.

♛ CONNECTIONS 8

The answers to these questions share a link . . . can you work out what it is?

1. A batter in baseball being awarded first base, and a batsman in cricket not waiting to be called out by the umpire do the same thing. What?
2. A Bombay duck is what type of creature?
3. Which Scottish football team are nicknamed 'The Tangerines'?
4. What is the only bird that can fly backwards?
5. Which antiquities were controversially removed from The Parthenon by Thomas Bruce between 1801 and 1812 and now reside in the British Museum in London?

What connection do these answers share?

Find out if you are right on page 209.

The Ministry of Quizzes asked 200 people in the UK: 'How long in miles is the Channel Tunnel?' This is how they responded:

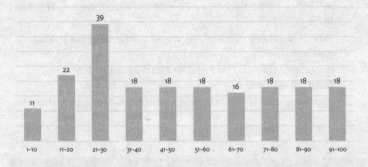

(For instance, 11 people gave an answer in the range of 1 and 10.*)

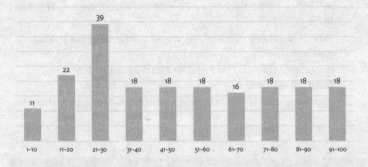 The middle answer	46	The most popular answer	30	The average answer	50
30.5	52	80	30
The middle answer from men	The middle answer from women	The most popular answer from people from the North	The most popular answer from people from the South

Based on this data, or otherwise, what is *your* estimate of the length of the Channel Tunnel?

The answer is on page 209.

* 4 people answered 'don't know'; their responses have not been included.

👑 JANE AUSTEN

How many questions on the topic of Jane Austen can you answer?

1. What was Jane Austen's first novel?
2. Which Jane Austen character has been played by Kate Beckinsale and Gwyneth Paltrow?
3. With whom does Lydia Bennet elope?
4. Which novel was Jane Austen writing at the time of her death?
5. Who did Jane Austen replace on the Bank of England £10 note in 2017?
6. Who played Jane Austen in the 2007 film, *Becoming Jane*?
7. Who played Mrs Bennet in the 1995 BBC TV adaption of *Pride and Prejudice*?
8. Which Jane Austen novel was originally titled *Elinor and Marianne*?
9. Which novel tells the story of Fanny Price?
10. A pheromone, discovered by researchers at the University of Liverpool in 2010, was named after which Jane Austen character?

Turn to page 205 for the answers.

👑 CONNECTIONS 9

The answers to these questions share a link . . . what is it?

1. What is the unpleasant sensation of dizziness, often incorrectly used to mean a fear of heights?
2. Which is the largest city in the state of Illinois?
3. Which composer wrote 'Moonlight Sonata' for his student Julie Guicciardi?
4. Which term for a large urban area comes from Greek meaning 'mother city'?
5. Tapeworms, roundworms, mistletoe and vampire bats are examples of what?

What connection do these answers share?

Find out if you are right on page 200.

♛ ODD ONE OUT 7

Which is the odd one out in each of these lists, and why?

1. Femur, Fibula, Tibia, Radius, Patella.
2. Djibouti, Comoros, Vanuatu, Togo, Côte d'Ivoire.
3. *Celestina* (Pablo Picasso), *Orange and Red on Red* (Mark Rothko), *The Starry Night* (Vincent van Gogh), *Blue Nude II* (Henri Matisse), *A Bigger Splash* (David Hockney).
4. Elinor Dashwood, Miss Havisham, Abel Magwitch, Bill Sikes, Sam Weller.
5. Jennifer Aniston, Greta Thunberg, Chesley 'Sully' Sullenberger, Dennis Bergkamp.

Go to page 196 for the answers.

♛ PHOBIAS

Try to list the **10** most common phobias (according to worldatlas. com). Earn points for more obscure answers, lose points for incorrect answers.

Answers on page 193.

♛ IN COMMON 7

What do the terms or names in each of these lists have in common?

1. Bill Bailey, Carrie Fisher, Dwight York, David Sole, Shannon Elizabeth.
2. Emperor, Jedi, Crusade, Christmas.
3. 20 July 1969, 19 November 1969, 5 February 1971, 30 July 1971, 20 April 1972, 11 December 1972.
4. Windsor, Venice, Verona, Athens.
5. Guinea, Africa, Macedonia, Arab Emirates, Timor.

Go to page 185 for the answers.

Try to answer these miscellaneous questions.

1. In an alphabetical list of UK cities, which one is first?

2. What word links 'oil', 'mass' and 'cowboy'?

3. In *Friends*, what was the name of Ross's pet monkey?

4. What characteristic are Boris Johnson and Andrew Bonar Law the only British prime ministers to share to date?

5. What is an anechoic chamber free from?

6. The word for which number scores itself in Scrabble?

7. What fictional country is Black Panther from?

8. In the *Mayor of Casterbridge* what does Michael Henchard sell for five guineas?

9. What links naval architect Thomas Andrews Jr, Jimi Heselden, owner of Segway Inc., and Henry Smolinski, inventor of the flying car?

10. Which is the only US state not made up of counties, but instead divided into parishes?

11. What English word comes from a Tibetan phrase meaning 'rock bear'?

12. Which country gained independence from Denmark in 1944?

13. Which typical curry accompaniment has a name meaning 'queen of fragrance'?

14. Maud Horsham, the protagonist in Emma Healey's novel *Elizabeth is Missing*, suffers from what medical condition?

15. In September 1944, Helen Duncan became the last person in the UK to be imprisoned for what?

The answers are on page 190.

Try to pick the correct option for each of these questions.

1. What is the first word of the Magna Carta?

    A. In   **B.** John

    C. King   **D.** God

2. 'So baby pull me closer in the back seat of your Rover . . .'
    Who sang these words?

    A. The Chainsmokers   **B.** Billie Eilish

    C. Dua Lipa   **D.** Doja Cat

3. Where is the Isle of Purbeck?

    A. Essex   **B.** Kent

    C. Dorset   **D.** Northumberland

4. What British product was banned in Denmark in 2011?

    A. Branston Pickle   **B.** HP Sauce

    C. Marmite   **D.** Worcester Sauce

5. If a 'whole note' is the US name for a semibreve, what would
    a quarter note be called in the UK?

    A. Minim   **B.** Crotchet

    C. Quaver   **D.** Semiquaver

6. Which is NOT an event in the heptathlon?

    A. 200 metres   **B.** 400 metres

    C. Javelin throw   **D.** Shot put

See page 217 for the answers.

👑 MORE, LESS OR THE SAME? 3

Which of these is more, which is less . . . or are they the same?

1. Which has more people (in active play), **a football team** or a **baseball team**? Or are they the same?
2. Which were there more of, **UK prime ministers in the 1950s** or **UK prime ministers in the 2010s**? Or are they the same?
3. Which are there more of, **countries in Asia** or **countries in Africa**? Or are they the same?
4. Which has more moons, **Mars** or **Pluto**? Or are they the same?
5. Which are there more of, **metatarsal bones in the foot** or **metacarpal bones in the hand**? Or are they the same?

Turn to page 200 for the answers.

👑 ALIASES

These questions concern aliases and alter egos. How many do you know?

1. Which musician was known as Satchmo?
2. What is Diana Prince's alter ego?
3. Which literary character travelled under the name of Mr Underhill?
4. How is YouTuber Felix Arvid Ulf Kjellberg better known?
5. In *Breaking Bad* what is Walter White's underground alias?
6. How is Baroque artist Michelangelo Merisi better known?
7. What is the nickname of golfer Frank Urban Zoeller, Jr?
8. How is Stephanie Gregory, who was at the centre of a US political scandal in 2018, better known?
9. How is Billie O'Connell better known?
10. What series of children's books were written by Georges Remi?

See page 217 for the answers.

👑 CLUEDO ROOMS

Try to list the **10** rooms in the original Cluedo game (including the room where the murder cards are placed). Earn points for more obscure answers, lose points for incorrect answers.

The answers are on page 213.

👑 FOOTBALL

How many questions relating to football can you answer?

1. The Henri Delaunay Trophy is awarded to the winner of which competition?
2. Which English Premiership team shares its name with a character in Shakespeare's *Henry IV Part 1*?
3. Megan Rapinoe captained which national football team?
4. Which goalkeeper to date has the most clean sheets in the English Premiership?
5. Three German clubs have won the European Cup/Champions League: Bayern Munich, Borussia Dortmund and which other?
6. Which player suffered a cardiac arrest at Euro 2020?
7. Denmark won the European Championship in 1992 despite not qualifying, which team did they replace?
8. Which outfield player has played in a Champions League final in three different decades?
9. Which winner of the Ballon d'Or went on to become president of an African country?
10. The highest attendance record for a premiership game, of 82,222, was set on 10 February 2018 at which stadium?

Find the answers on page 209.

Arrange the items in each of these lists in the correct order.

1. Starting with the fewest, arrange these 3D shapes according to the number of faces.

    - Cube
    - Octahedron
    - Triangular prism
    - Dodecahedron
    - Tetrahedron

2. Starting with the smallest, arrange these bodies of water in the English Lake District in order of area.

    - Buttermere
    - Rydal Water
    - Windermere
    - Coniston Water
    - Ullswater

3. Starting with the earliest, put these artists in order of when they lived and worked.

    - Mark Rothko
    - Sandro Botticelli
    - Vincent van Gogh
    - Rembrandt
    - Thomas Gainsborough

4. Starting with the fewest, arrange these artists in order of how many members they each have in their standard line-up.

    - Arcade Fire
    - The Killers
    - Madness
    - Destiny's Child
    - Kool and the Gang

The answers are on page 206.

👑 WHAT COMES NEXT? 6

Who or what comes next in each of these sequences?

1. Genesis, Exodus, Leviticus, Numbers . . .?
2. Caught, bowled, LBW, run out . . .?
3. C, D, I, L, M . . .?
4. Burj Khalifa, Taipei 101, Petronas Towers, Sears Tower . . .?
5. Bi, Tr, Ob, Bu, Cl, Bu . . .?

See page 205 for the answers.

👑 LETTER BOX 4

The clues correspond to single letters. The letters make a coiled-up, 9-letter word. The word can start in any square, and can run in any direction, but always through adjacent squares. Solve the clues to unscramble the word.

Clue: Fast-growing, source of boundary disputes.

Ron Hubbard	14 in hexadecimal	Vertical axis
Should cocoa	2015 Grammy winning Kendrick Lamar song	Plate on a learner vehicle
Five hundred Romans	SI unit for force	Note an orchestra tunes up to

The answers are on page 196.

Try to pick the correct option for each of these questions.

1. Who had a hit in 2018 with 'Sicko Mode'?

   A. Juice Wrld   **B.** Shawn Mendes

   C. Sia   **D.** Travis Scott

2. Which of these England footballers was not knighted?

   A. Bobby Moore   **B.** Bobby Charlton

   C. Geoff Hurst   **D.** Stanley Matthews

3. What is the collective noun for unicorns?

   A. Blessing   **B.** Treasure

   C. Treat   **D.** Windfall

4. Approximately how long does it take for light from the Sun to arrive at the Earth?

   A. 8 seconds   **B.** 8 minutes

   C. 8 hours   **D.** 8 days

5. In the Harry Potter film series, which of these characters is NOT played by Warwick Davis?

   A. Professor Flitwick   **B.** Griphook

   C. Goblin Bank Teller   **D.** Kreacher

6. Who did Angela Merkel succeed as German Chancellor?

   A. Helmut Kohl   **B.** Gerhard Schröder

   C. Helmut Schmidt   **D.** Willy Brandt

The answers are on page 193.

These questions refer to the elements pictured with their symbols and atomic numbers. Some questions may give you clues to the answers to others. Use this – and your knowledge, of course – to work out as many of their identities as you can . . . and answer the questions.

1. Which *five* are gases at room temperature?
2. Which *two* are liquid at room temperature?
3. Which *two* are radioactive?
4. Which *three* have four-letter names?
5. Which *three* are named after or share their names with planets?
6. The name of which derives from the Latin hydrargyrum, meaning 'liquid silver'?
7. Which is the symbol of a 50-year anniversary?
8. Which *three* occur naturally in the atmosphere?
9. Which *three* together make up both alcohol and sugar molecules?
10. Which makes up around 12% of the mass of all plants and around 20% of the mass of all animals?
11. Which *two* make up table salt?
12. Which is the lightest (which has the smallest atomic mass)?
13. Which is put in swimming pools to eliminate bacteria and algae?
14. Which of these is the best conductor of electricity and is used extensively to make electric cables?
15. Which glows in the dark?
16. Which of these is the least chemically reactive?

The solution is on page 189.

8 **O** A.	80 **Hg** B.	15 **P** C.	30 **Zn** D.
35 **Br** E.	6 **C** F.	92 **U** G.	18 **Ar** H.
82 **Pb** I.	1 **H** J.	17 **Cl** K.	79 **Au** L.
94 **Pu** M.	29 **Cu** N.	7 **N** O.	11 **Na** P.

Try to answer these miscellaneous questions.

1. Published in 1994, *Closing Time* was the follow-up to which bestselling 1961 novel?

2. The German word 'stachelschwein', literally meaning 'spike pig', is equivalent to what word in English?

3. After the Sahara and the Arabian what is the third-largest true desert in the world?

4. Exposure to what causes skunked beer?

5. Mel Blanc, the voice of Bugs Bunny, Daffy Duck, Porky Pig, Tweety Pie and many other classic cartoon characters, died in 1989. What three-word phrase did he ask to have on his gravestone?

6. The word 'phone' can be made from the chemical symbols of which four elements?

7. What is the world's oldest continually inhabited city?

8. Which Christian festival comes nine months after the Annunciation?

9. No simian shaken up and staying awake? (anag, 8)

10. Which team did Michael Jordan play for?

11. 'I heard that you're settled down' is the first line of what song?

12. Chinook, Sundowner, Levant and Mistral are all types of what?

13. How many litres are there in a Magnum (of Champagne)?

14. (In the play) what are Vladimir and Estragon doing?

15. 'Half the World Away' by Oasis is the theme music to which British TV comedy?

See page 185 for the answers.

Find each answer using the clues in turn – the least number of clues the better.

1. Who is this?

   - She was born Ruth Elizabeth but took her stage name from an Honoré de Balzac novel.
   - Susan Sarandon played her in the docudrama TV series *Feud*, about her rivalry with Joan Crawford.
   - She starred in *Jezebel* (1938), *All About Eve* (1950) and *What Ever Happened to Baby Jane?* (1962).
   - She was namechecked in a 1981 hit song by Kim Carnes.

2. Who is this?

   - Formed by munitions workers in 1886 under the name 'Dial Square' in reference to the sundial on top of the entrance to the factory.
   - Their first home was Plumstead Common in South East London.
   - They were the first club in the south of England to join the Football League.
   - Their 'Invincibles' team holds the record to date for the longest run of league matches unbeaten – 49 games from 7 May 2003 to 24 October 2004.

3. When (what year) is this?

   - The Øresund Bridge between Denmark and Sweden opens to traffic.
   - Concorde crashes on take-off in Paris and all Concorde flights are immediately suspended.
   - George Bush defeats Al Gore in the US presidential election, the result comes down to disputed votes – infamous 'hanging chads' – in Florida.
   - Fears of worldwide failures to computer systems prove unfounded.

See page 221 for the answers.

The answers to these questions share a link . . . can you work out what it is?

1. What is the nickname of Sunderland FC?
2. Which biblical prophet was swallowed by a giant fish?
3. Which Shakespeare character was described as being 'full of the milk of human kindness'?
4. How is Rossini's opera *La Gazza Ladra* better known in English?
5. Which is the smallest prime number that makes another, different, prime number when its digits are reversed?

What connection do these answers share?

Find out if you are right on page 217.

Find out if you are right on page 217.

👑 FIFTY-FIFTY 10

Try to answer these fifty-fifty questions.

1. In which fantasy series is there a character called Fredegar Bolger, **Game of Thrones** or **The Lord of the Rings**?
2. What religion were the French Huguenots, **Catholic** or **Protestant**?
3. Into which ocean does the greater total volume of river water flow, the **Atlantic** or the **Pacific**?
4. Whose 2013 tour was called the 'Mrs Carter Show', **Beyoncé** or **Lady Gaga**?
5. How much is a dime, **five cents** or **ten cents**?

Turn to page 213 for the answers.

The Ministry of Quizzes asked 200 people in the UK: *'How many keys in total – black and white – are there on a standard piano keyboard?'* This is how they responded:

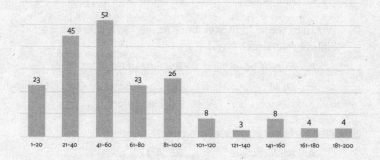

(For instance, 23 people gave an answer in the range of 1 and 20.*)

The middle answer	52	The most popular answer	88	The average answer	63

50	52	52	88
The middle answer from men	The middle answer from women	The most popular answer from people aged over 30	The most popular answer from people aged 30 and under

Based on this data, or otherwise, what is *your* estimate of the number of keys on a piano keyboard?

The answer is on page 209.

* 4 people answered 'don't know'; their responses have not been included.

Try to pick the correct option for each of these questions.

1. Which country do gerbils come from?
    - **A.** India
    - **B.** Mexico
    - **C.** Mongolia
    - **D.** Peru

2. Which of these John Steinbeck novels has a title that is a biblical reference?
    - **A.** *Cup of Gold*
    - **B.** *East of Eden*
    - **C.** *Of Mice and Men*
    - **D.** *The Winter of Our Discontent*

3. What is featured on all Euro notes?
    - **A.** Architecture
    - **B.** Art
    - **C.** Notable Europeans
    - **D.** Landscapes

4. Which UK city is served by Ringway Airport?
    - **A.** Bristol
    - **B.** Manchester
    - **C.** Newcastle
    - **D.** Glasgow

5. The inferior vena cava is the largest what in the human body?
    - **A.** Artery
    - **B.** Gland
    - **C.** Nerve
    - **D.** Vein

6. What does framboise mean in French cooking?
    - **A.** Cooked with flame
    - **B.** Cream cake
    - **C.** Raspberry
    - **D.** Marinade

Answers on page 205.

The clues in the grid relate to the numbers 1 to 9. No number is repeated. Use a process of elimination to work out which number is which.

Square feet in a square yard	Borders of South Korea with other countries	Decimal equivalent of 1,000 in binary
Names in '50 Ways to Leave Your Lover'	Points for the letter 'C' in Scrabble	Square segments in each block in Tetris
Violinists in a string quartet	Players in a netball team	Countries larger in area than India

Go to page 200 for the solution.

♔ MORE, LESS OR THE SAME? 4

Which of these is more, which is less . . . or are they the same?

1. Which is larger, **3 x 5!** or **3⁵**? Or are they the same?
2. Which are there more of, Agatha Christie novels featuring **Miss Marple** or Agatha Christie novels featuring **Hercule Poirot**? Or are they the same?
3. Which is more, years since the **formation of the EU** (the signing of the Maastricht Treaty) or years since the **end of apartheid** in South Africa? Or are they the same?
4. Who was older (in years) when they died, **Buddy Holly** or **Tupac Shakur**? Or were they the same?
5. Which are there more of on the Stars and Stripes, **red stripes** or **white stripes**? Or are they the same?

See page 221 for the answers.

MATCHING PAIRS: ANAGRAMS OF BRITISH FOOTBALL TEAMS

Can you match the team to its anagram? (For a harder game, and more points, play 'blind' without the answers in the second grid.)

1. Neon Toiletry	2. Unedited Nude	3. Twopenny Court	4. Earwax Calendar
5. Thrash Mutton Poet	6. Chicory Twin	7. Insects Away	8. Travel Op
9. Enacted Wine Lust	10. Sticky Toe	11. Ruinous Themes	12. Ticklish Patter

A. Newport County	B. Port Vale	C. Norwich City	D. Leyton Orient
E. Stenhouse-muir	F. Stoke City	G. Dundee United	H. Tottenham Hotspur
I. Partick Thistle	J. Swansea City	K. Newcastle United	L. Crewe Alexandra

The solution is on page 193.

👑 ODDS AND ENDS 17

Try to answer these miscellaneous questions.

1. Which successful US recording artist has a surname of Dutch origin, which literally translates as 'jumping stone'?
2. What type of animal is a 'deathstalker'?
3. What county is John O'Groats in?
4. 'Cor' in Latin, 'kardia' in Greek, what is it in English?
5. In the film *The Great Escape*, what was the codename of the tunnel through which the final breakout was made?
6. Berry hubs rummaging around in a garden feature? (anag, 9)
7. What colour is at the top of a rainbow?
8. Which figure in mythology controversially killed King Laius and married Queen Jocasta?
9. Which two Asian countries, once connected by a land bridge, have since 1480 been separated by the Palk Strait?
10. The George Cross was created in 1940 primarily to honour acts of bravery by who?
11. High lyric pose deciphered a symbolic language? (anag, 13)
12. Alan Partridge's catchphrase uses which ABBA song?
13. How many compartments can the ball land in on a standard roulette wheel?
14. Which four letters were emblematic of the Roman Republic?
15. What name links cricketer William Gilbert, actor Kelly and singer Jones?

Find the answers on page 189.

👑 ODD ONE OUT 8

Which is the odd one out in each of these lists, and why?

1. Sheep, hound, biscuit, shaggy, police.
2. Ankara, Beijing, Brasilia, Ottawa, Paris.
3. *The Hangover, Iron Man, Rocky, Inception, The Bourne Identity*.
4. John F. Kennedy, Ronald Reagan, George Bush, Bill and Hillary Clinton, Donald Trump.
5. Alice, the Dormouse, the Hatter, the March Hare, the Queen of Hearts.

Answers on page 185.

👑 INSECTS

These questions relate to insects. How many can you answer?

1. Atlas, Gypsy and Garden Tiger are types of what insect?
2. What is the young of a damselfly called?
3. What is the middle section of an insect's body?
4. What is the figure-of-eight movement honeybees make to communicate the location of pollen?
5. Someone who practises entomophagy does what to insects?
6. What type of insect is a whirligig?
7. Which insect can run the fastest?
8. What insect might secrete 'Royal Jelly'?
9. What insect species has the name 'religiosa'?
10. How is Stuart Goddard better known?

The answers are on page 196.

Try to pick the correct option for each of these questions.

1. Which book was subtitled 'A Pure Woman Faithfully Presented'?

    A. *Tess of the d'Urbervilles*   **B.** *Jane Eyre*

    C. *Emma*   **D.** *Anna Karenina*

2. The modernist architect who designed London's Trellick Tower shares his surname with which James Bond villain?

    A. Blofeld   **B.** Drax

    C. Goldfinger   **D.** Trevelyan

3. Where is the Ashmolean Museum?

    A. Cambridge   **B.** Edinburgh

    C. Glasgow   **D.** Oxford

4. Which Spice Girl's first solo hit was 'Not Such An Innocent Girl'?

    A. Baby   **B.** Ginger

    C. Posh   **D.** Sporty

5. Hydroponics is the method of growing plants without what?

    A. Soil   **B.** Water

    C. Light   **D.** Air

6. Which driver did Lewis Hamilton replace when he joined Mercedes in 2013?

    A. Rubens Barrichello   **B.** Fernando Alonso

    C. Michael Schumacher   **D.** Sebastian Vettel

Find the answers on page 217.

The clues in the grid correspond to numbers. The rows, columns and the two diagonals add up to the same number – the Magic Number. Use the clues to find this Magic Number and solve the grid!

Clue to the Magic Number: 5! - (4! + 2!)

2^4 x 3	Strings on a violin	*Steps*	Little pigs
Strokes needed to make a 147 break	Sides on a standard pencil	Five times the sum of its digits	Different husbands of Elizabeth Taylor
Seasons of *Game of Thrones*	Furry foot (anag)	Score for a birdie	Beans in every cup of Nescafé
Only even prime number	Number with letters in alphabetical order	Players in a (field) hockey team	Country code for Switzerland

The solution is on page 213.

👑 THE ANCIENT WORLD

Try to answer these questions on the ancient world.

1. What event took place for the first time in 776 BC?
2. Who did Caesar cross the Rubicon to fight?
3. Which city state did Athens fight in the Peloponnesian Wars?
4. In Rome, 69 AD was the year of four what?
5. What, in 1964, happened to the 3,200-year-old statues and temples at Abu Simbel in Egypt?
6. Which Greek philosopher wrote *The Republic*?
7. Which ancient Greek writer is known as the Father of History?
8. Which sea-faring civilization is credited with inventing the alphabet?
9. The precise location of which of the Seven Wonders of the Ancient World is unknown?
10. In which modern country is the ancient city of Carthage?

See page 209 for the answers.

👑 FIFTY-FIFTY II

Try to answer these fifty-fifty questions.

1. How did Michael Chang unsettle Ivan Lendl on his way to winning the 1989 French Open, did he **play left-handed** or **serve underarm**?
2. Gymnophobia is the fear of what, **horses** or **nudity**?
3. Which art and design movement came earlier, **Art Deco** or **Art Nouveau**?
4. How long was the Thirty Years War, **30 years** or **not 30 years**?
5. In Ireland, cars drive on which side of the road, the **left** or the **right**?

Go to page 192 for the answers.

Try to answer these miscellaneous questions.

1. In the Harry Potter series, what is the name of Hermione's cat?

2. In which sport in the Summer Olympics do competitors 'transition'?

3. Who sang the opening line of 'We are the World' (by USA for Africa)?

4. Better bang mixture to make this cake? (anag, 10)

5. What feat was first achieved by cosmonaut Alexei Leonov in 1965?

6. What shop was first opened by Ingvar Kamprad in Älmhult, Småland, in 1958?

7. Which city in the Midlands shares its postcode with a blood group?

8. In the chorus of 'Waltzing Matilda', the swagman is waiting for what to boil?

9. What song is Bill Murray repeatedly woken up to in *Groundhog Day*?

10. The title of which aria from a Puccini opera means 'none shall sleep'?

11. A Black and Tan is a mixture of pale ale and what other drink?

12. Kate Moss has a tattoo of two swallows at the base of her back, created by which well-known artist?

13. What is notable about a point on the Rhine-Main-Danube-Canal in Bavaria, between the Hilpoltstein and Bachhausen?

14. In what order do The Beatles cross Abbey Road?

15. Which vegetable family does the herb coriander belong to?

Answers on page 205.

👑 AFRICA

How many questions on the subject of Africa can you answer?

1. Which city is situated at the confluence of the White Nile and the Blue Nile?
2. 'Release iron' is an anagram of which African country?
3. Which nation has won the Africa Cup of Nations the most times?
4. Which African country has a capital named after a US President?
5. What links Ras ben Sakka in Tunisia, Ras Hafun in Somalia, Cape Agulhas in South Africa and Cap Vert in Senegal?
6. The name for what popular game comes from the Swahili word for 'to build'?
7. Which African leader was known as 'Madiba'?
8. What is the longest African river that flows into the Indian Ocean?
9. 'Dough aims' is an anagram of which African city?
10. In the Toto song, what time is the flight she is coming in on?

Find the answers on page 196.

👑 CONNECTIONS II

The answers to these questions share a link . . . what is it?

1. In Formula 1, what colour flag indicates that a driver has been disqualified?
2. Which British glam rock band had a hit in 2003 with 'I Believe in a Thing Called Love'?
3. What was Iran called prior to 1935?
4. In which London park is London Zoo located?
5. In which part of the UK are Pontarddulais, Tonypandy and Harlech?

What connection do these answers share?

Find out if you are right on page 212.

The Ministry of Quizzes asked 200 people in the UK: *'How fast was Usain Bolt travelling in miles per hour when he set the 100m world record in 2009?'* This is how they responded:

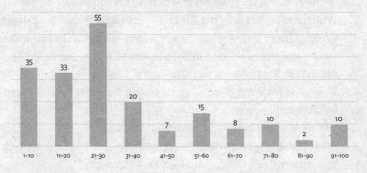

(For instance, 35 people gave an answer in the range of 1 and 10.*)

The middle answer **27**	The most popular answer **20**	The average answer **34**

25	**30**	**25**	**29**
The middle answer from people from the North	The middle answer from people from the South	The most popular answer from men	The most popular answer from women

Based on this data, or otherwise, what is *your* estimate of the speed of Usain Bolt when he broke the world 100m record?

The answer is on page 185.

* 5 people answered 'don't know'; their responses have not been included.

👑 WHAT COMES NEXT? 7

Who or what comes next in each of these sequences?

1. Door, anymore, goodbye, die . . .?
2. £60, £60, £200, £100, £100 . . .?
3. PS, COS, POA, GOF, OOTP . . .?
4. Donut, reign, miaow, farce, solar, latte . . .?
5. Born, christened, married, took ill . . .?

Go to page 189 for the answers.

👑 ABUNDANT CHEMICAL ELEMENTS

Try to list the **10** most abundant chemical elements in the universe. Earn points for more obscure answers, lose points for incorrect answers.

Find the answers on page 217.

👑 IN COMMON 8

What do the terms in each of these lists have in common?

1. *Major League, Witchfinder General, A Private Function, The French Lieutenant's Woman.*
2. Hampshire, York, Jersey, Mexico.
3. The Duke of Wellington, George Stephenson, Elizabeth Fry, Winston Churchill.
4. Pink Floyd, ABBA, The Flying Lizards, Dire Straits, Simply Red.
5. Kuwait, Mexico, Guatemala, Panama.

Go to page 220 for the answers.

Find each answer using the clues in turn – the least number of clues the better.

1. What is this?
   - She measured 787 feet long, 87 feet wide and 165 feet high.
   - She was named after a Roman province located in modern Portugal.
   - From 1907 until 1909 she held the Blue Riband, that is, the record for the fastest transatlantic crossing.
   - She was torpedoed by a German U-boat off the southern coast of Ireland in 1916, contributing to the United States' entry into World War I.

2. Where is this?
   - It is situated on the Vltava River.
   - It has the oldest working astronomical clock in the world.
   - It was the centre of the Velvet Revolution in 1989.
   - It is the historical capital of Bohemia.

3. What is this?
   - It is caused by the variola virus.
   - Rameses V is thought to have died from this disease.
   - The vaccine against this disease, pioneered by Edward Jenner, was the first ever to be developed against a contagious disease.
   - It was eradicated in 1979, the successful result of a global vaccination programme by the World Health Organization.

Find the answers on page 213.

Try to pick the correct option for each of these questions.

1. Who framed Roger Rabbit?
   - **A.** Judge Doom
   - **B.** Marvin Acme
   - **C.** Baby Herman
   - **D.** Jessica Rabbit

2. Which novel is subtitled 'A Study of Provincial Life'?
   - **A.** *Cider with Rosie*
   - **B.** *The Darling Buds of May*
   - **C.** *Middlemarch*
   - **D.** *The Mill on the Floss*

3. What was the first rap/hip hop song to win an Academy Award?
   - **A.** 'Can I Get A . . .' (Jay-Z)
   - **B.** 'Gangsta's Paradise' (Coolio)
   - **C.** 'Lose Yourself' (Eminem)
   - **D.** 'Paper Planes' (M.I.A.)

4. Which of these countries is furthest from where guinea pigs actually come from?
   - **A.** Guinea
   - **B.** Guinea-Bissau
   - **C.** Equatorial Guinea
   - **D.** Papua New Guinea

5. Pedology is the study of what?
   - **A.** Feet
   - **B.** Soil
   - **C.** Children
   - **D.** Palm reading

6. Fray Bentos, a brand name best known for meat pies, is a town in which country?
   - **A.** Argentina
   - **B.** Ireland
   - **C.** Spain
   - **D.** Uruguay

Find the answers on page 208.

Match these song lyrics to the places in the pictures. Earn bonus points for knowing the songs and the artists.

1.	2.	3.
You were handsome, you were pretty, Queen of _____	If you can use some exotic booze, there's a bar in far _____	All you need's a strong heart and a nerve of steel, Viva _____
4.	**5.**	**6.**
Are you going to _____ fair? Parsley, sage, rosemary and thyme	I'm heading down the _____ highway, looking for the love getaway	New York, London, Paris, _____, everybody talk about pop muzik
7.	**8.**	**9.**
Way on down south, way on down south _____ town	This ain't no disco, it ain't no country club either, this is _____	Don't you know that _____ wasn't built in a day
10.	**11.**	**12.**
Coast to coast, LA to _____, western male	I was sick and tired of everything when I called you last night from _____	Every gal in Constantinople lives in _____ not Constantinople

A.

B.

C.

D.

E.

F.

G.

H.

I.

J.

K.

L.

Go to page 204 for the solution.

Try to answer these miscellaneous questions.

1. How many full stops are there in the novel *Solar Bones* by Mike McCormack?

2. The name of which fictional teen character had to be changed after it was discovered the character's intended name 'Alexis Texas' was used by an adult film actress?

3. What does a vexillologist study?

4. What word for a geographical feature comes from Latin meaning 'almost an island'?

5. What world city with a population greater than 1 million people is the furthest in the world from the next nearest city with a population over 1 million?

6. What French term means 'cooked in pastry'?

7. What phrase did court officials use to instruct the Tower of London to bring to trial those accused of treason, giving the title to a book by Hilary Mantel?

8. In Japan, 'karoshi' is a death caused by what?

9. What is the fruit of the blackthorn?

10. Sirimavo Bandaranaike was elected prime minister of which country in 1960, becoming the world's first democratically elected female leader?

11. Brute tech reassembled a medieval weapon? (anag, 9)

12. Who once gave Marilyn Monroe a poodle called Mafia?

13. Who was controversially awarded the Turner Prize in 2019?

14. The Marconi company first defined it as 'CQD' in 1904, but it soon became universally adopted as what three letters?

15. In science fiction, what is a 'Voight-Kampff' test designed to reveal?

Find the answers on page 200.

👑 FIFTY-FIFTY 12

Try to answer these fifty-fifty questions.

1. BTS are what genre of music, **J-Pop** or **K-Pop**?
2. Which weighs more, **two 1p coins** or **one 10p coin**?
3. Which is larger, a **basketball court** or a **netball court**?
4. Entomophobia is the fear of what, **insects** or **words**?
5. Which pantomime is the story of a boy and a resourceful cat he inherits from his father, *Puss in Boots* or *Dick Whittington*?

Go to page 196 for the answers.

👑 CONNECTIONS 12

The answers to these questions share a link . . . can you work out what it is?

1. Which 2014 science-fiction film about a humanlike, intelligent robot starred Domhnall Gleeson, Alicia Vikander and Oscar Isaac?
2. What word goes with 'road', 'nose' and 'numerals'?
3. Which Shakespeare comedy, with a title meaning an inappropriate amount of fuss, is set in Messina in Sicily?
4. How is 'self-contained underwater breathing apparatus' more commonly known?
5. In the US it's a cab stand, what is it in the UK?

What connection do these answers share?

Find out if you are right on page 192.

Work out the links between the answers to the questions to solve the grid. Use the grid to help you answer all the questions.

2 Across (7 letters)

1. Who played the eponymous role in *Spartacus* in 1960?

2. What name is given to a vertical column of elements in the periodic table?

3. What hard, glass-like rock occurs in chalk or limestone rock formations, and has been used to make tools and start fires?

4. Which fish is used in Arbroath smokie?

5. What small, thin chilli pepper used extensively in Southeast Asian cooking is hotter than a jalapeno but not as hot as a habanero?

. . . what is the link?

3 Across (6)

1. What facial feature is sometimes called the supercilium?
2. The English word 'plumber' derives from the Latin name for which metal?
3. In language, nominative, accusative, genitive and dative are types of what?
4. What is the part of a hovercraft that inflates with air?
5. Ace mouths with this hairy appendage? (anag, 9)

. . . what is the link?

1 Down (5)

1. What American state is known as the 'Golden State'?
2. Which ship carried pilgrims from Plymouth to the New World in 1620?
3. Which winter vegetable, named after a region in France, has characteristic green, crinkled leaves?
4. On which English town is Hardy's *The Mayor of Casterbridge* based?
5. Far self jumbled-up charity prize draws? (anag, 7)

. . . what is the link?

2 Down (7)

1. What can be a mountainous feature or an urban slang term for a large group of people, bigger than a crew or posse?
2. What title is shared by different hit songs by Simon and Garfunkel and Razorlight?
3. In geometry, what is an entity that has a location in space or on a plane, but no extent?
4. Overran site wrongly enclosing native population? (anag, 11)
5. Where in the UK would you find Pacific Quay, the SEC Armadillo, and the Clyde Arc?

. . . what is the link?

Find the solution on page 188.

Who or what comes next in each of these sequences?

1. Russia, Canada, United States, China . . .?
2. Cesar Romero, Jack Nicholson, Heath Ledger, Cameron Monaghan, Jared Leto . . .?
3. 8, 5, 4, 9, 1, 7 . . .?
4. Rwanda, Tanzania, Uganda, South Sudan, Sudan . . .?
5. Deacon, Priest, Bishop, Archbishop . . .?

Answers on page 184.

TECHNOLOGY

These questions all relate to technology. How many can you answer?

1. What strong material was invented by Stephanie Kwolek in 1965?
2. Which car manufacturer invented the three-point seatbelt, allowing the design to be used by others for free?
3. *Unua Libro* was the first book written in which language?
4. What was invented by Thomas Twyford?
5. In computing, what does USB stand for?
6. Who took the crystal photographs that were instrumental in Watson and Crick deducing the structure of DNA?
7. Which was the first Asian nation to put a spacecraft in orbit around Mars?
8. Which motor company was named after the daughter of an automobile pioneer?
9. How is the technology company Lucky Goldstar better known?
10. What term for problem solving is often attributed to Grace Hopper in the 1940s after she discovered a moth in a relay in the computer she was working on?

Go to page 220 for the answers.

Try to answer these miscellaneous questions.

1. Which athlete, nicknamed the 'Maputo Express', competed at six summer Olympic Games, winning gold in Sydney in 2000 in the women's 800m?

2. Where in the UK might residents be affectionately called 'Smoggies'?

3. 'Baby's Breath', 'Bird of Paradise' and 'Red hot poker' are all types of what?

4. Which building, designed by architect Jørn Utzon, did Clive James once describe as a 'Nun's Scrum'?

5. Which Pixar film features a golden retriever called Dug?

6. Countries from which continent boycotted the 1966 FIFA World Cup?

7. What was notable about Tom Hanks's Oscar wins for *Philadelphia* and *Forrest Gump* that has, as of 2021, not happened since?

8. Which continent makes up 9% of the Earth's surface?

9. With which opera singer did Freddie Mercury duet on the song 'Barcelona'?

10. Dream-spin entangled this hybrid character? (anag, 6-3)

11. Eustatic change refers to global rises or falls in what?

12. Referred to by its builders as the 'Anti-Fascist Protection Rampart', how was it better known?

13. In the original game of Cluedo, which room has the fewest letters?

14. Taming her frightfully bad dream? (anag, 9)

15. 'As far back as I can remember I always wanted to be a gangster' is the first line of which movie?

The answers are on page 216.

LONDON UNDERGROUND STATIONS BEGINNING WITH 'L'

Try to list the **10** stations on the London Underground that begin with the letter 'L'. Earn points for more obscure answers, lose points for incorrect answers.

Answers on page 213.

 # ODD ONE OUT 9

Which is the odd one out in each of these lists, and why?

1. Plum, Cherry, Banana, Ruby, Beef.
2. Erie, Huron, Winnipeg, Michigan, Ontario.
3. Olly Murs, Alexandra Burke, Susan Boyle, Leona Lewis.
4. *Adam Bede, Barnaby Rudge, Daniel Deronda, Silas Marner.*
5. Mars, Twix, Crunchie, Bounty, Snickers.

Turn to page 208 for the answers.

IN COMMON 9

What do the terms in each of these lists have in common?

1. Albert Einstein, Dmitri Mendeleyev, Marie Curie, Thor, Neptune.
2. Southern, Australian, Swiss, Maritime.
3. *The House at Pooh Corner*, the 'King of the Blues', the first iron steamship to cross the Atlantic, Frank Beard/Dusty Hill/ Billy Gibbons.
4. Mary Pickford, Rob Roy, Tom Collins, Mary Tudor.
5. Jack, Henry, Dick, Columbus.

Turn to page 204 for the answers.

Try to pick the correct option for each of these questions.

1. In Shakespeare's *Henry V*, what gift does the Dauphin bring Henry?

    A. His niece's hand in marriage

    B. A horse

    C. Wine

    D. Tennis balls

2. What colour is zaffre?

    A. Blue

    B. Black

    C. Red

    D. Yellow

3. Billingsgate Market in London is best known for what?

    A. Fish

    B. Flowers

    C. Fruit and vegetables

    D. Meat

4. Which of these historical events was NOT mentioned in Billy Joel's 'We Didn't Start the Fire'?

    A. The Bay of Pigs

    B. Watergate

    C. The Fall of the Berlin Wall

    D. The AIDS pandemic

5. What is a 'moneywort'?

    A. A debt

    B. A flowering plant

    C. An insect

    D. An entrepreneur

6. Which country finished second in the medal table at the Rio Olympics in 2016?

    A. China

    B. Great Britain

    C. Russia

    D. The United States

Turn to page 199 for the answers.

THE WISDOM OF THE CROWD: HADRIAN'S WALL

The Ministry of Quizzes asked 200 people in the UK: *'How long, in miles, was Hadrian's Wall?'* This is how they responded:

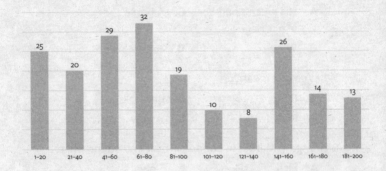

(For instance, 25 people gave an answer in the range of 1 and 20.*)

The middle answer **73**	The most popular answer **150**	The average answer **90**
70	**84**	**89**	**73**
The middle answer from people from the North	The middle answer from people from the South	The middle answer from people aged over 30	The middle answer from people aged 30 or under

Based on this data, or otherwise, what is *your* estimate of the length of Hadrian's Wall?

The answer is on page 195.

* 4 people answered 'don't know'; their responses have not been included.

Who or what comes next in each of these sequences?

1. Y, M, W, D, H, M . . .?
2. Captain Jonathan Archer, Captain Robert April, Captain Christopher Pike . . .?
3. Deci, Centi, Milli, Micro . . .?
4. Alabama, Alaska, Arizona, Arkansas . . .?
5. Bl, Pi, Bl, Gr, Br, Ye . . .?

Turn to page 192 for the answers.

👑 METEOROLOGY AND THE ATMOSPHERE

These questions concern meteorology and the atmosphere. How many can you answer?

1. What term refers to the amount of water vapour in the air?
2. What is the line on a weather chart that joins points of equal pressure?
3. The Beaufort Scale is a twelve-point scale used to describe what?
4. What gas makes up 21% of the Earth's atmosphere?
5. What is a haboob?
6. Above what wind speed, in metres per second, are times set in sprint or jump events in international athletics deemed illegal?
7. An okta is a measure of what meteorological observation?
8. Expose her circulating in the outer atmosphere? (anag, 9)
9. What name was given to the hurricane that, in 2005, brought widespread flooding to Louisiana and is to date the most financially costly in US history?
10. Meaning 'baby' in Spanish, what is the cyclical climate phenomenon affecting long-term weather patterns in the Pacific region?

Find the answers on page 188.

👑 CONNECTIONS 13

The answers to these questions share a link . . . can you work out what it is?

1. What word goes with 'private', 'teeth' and 'candy'?
2. In what type of paddled vessel did Ed McKeever and Liam Heath win gold medals for Great Britain in the London and Rio Olympics, respectively?
3. The correct form of address for the Queen is 'Your Majesty' at the first address and subsequently what thereafter?
4. In Indian cooking, what is a leavened bread typically served as an accompaniment to a meal?
5. What is the common, trademarked name for a self-propelled garden cultivating machine?

What connection do these answers share?

Find out if you are right on page 184.

👑 IN COMMON 10

What do the terms in each of these lists have in common?

1. *Mamma Mia!, Avengers: Endgame, Once Upon a Time . . . In Hollywood, Kick-Ass, What Ever Happened to Baby Jane?.*
2. Lyme, Grafton, Milton, Brompton, Bere.
3. Upper cut, wash-out, cabbage patch, nervous nineties, pyjamas.
4. Ration, apex, foxglove, bathing, coward.
5. Austria, Chad, Laos, Paraguay, Switzerland.

The answers are on page 220.

Try to answer these miscellaneous questions.

1. Crème de Cassis is made from which fruit?

2. What was Monica Ali's first novel?

3. Of the canon of popular pantomimes, which is the only one based on a true story?

4. Merited drinks cocktail in UK town? (anag, 13)

5. In darts, what score is known as a 'devil'?

6. British publisher Ludvik Hoch was better known by which name?

7. In which movie does a character say the words 'Back, and to the left . . . back, and to the left . . . back, and to the left'?

8. Kaolin is an industrial raw material used among other things in the production of paper. Its name derives from Gaoling in China, where it was used to make porcelain. How is it commonly known?

9. Who is the oldest person to have appeared on a UK number one single?

10. Who succeeded Nelson Mandela as president of South Africa?

11. Where in the UK might residents affectionately be called 'Loiners'?

12. Marko Ramius captained which fictional vessel?

13. What bridge connects Dawes Point to Milsons Point?

14. In what song do we hear the words 'Fill up my cup, Mazel Tov'?

15. Which racecourse is considered the headquarters of British horse racing?

Go to page 216 for the answers.

Arrange the items in each of these lists in the correct order.

1. Starting with the earliest, arrange these nations in order of when they first won the FIFA World Cup.
   - Brazil
   - France
   - Spain
   - Uruguay
   - West Germany

2. Starting with the earliest, arrange these twentieth-century movies in order of when they were released.
   - *The Deer Hunter*
   - *The Godfather*
   - *Raiders of the Lost Ark*
   - *Rocky*
   - *The Sound of Music*

3. Starting with the smallest, arrange these lakes in order of area.
   - The Caspian Sea
   - Lake Erie
   - Lake Michigan
   - Lake Victoria
   - Lake Titicaca

4. Starting with the smallest (i.e. the most recent), arrange these species in order of how long they have been on the Earth.
   - Bears
   - Bees
   - Jellyfish
   - Sharks
   - Whales

Answers on page 212.

Try to pick the correct option for each of these questions.

1. What song begins with the lyric: 'Sí, sabes que ya llevo un rato mirándote, tengo que bailar contigo hoy'?

   A. 'Bamboléo' **B.** 'Despacito'

   C. 'Volver a Empezar' **D.** 'Fernando'

2. Who wrote the short story *The Curious Case of Benjamin Button*?

   A. F. Scott Fitzgerald **B.** Truman Capote

   C. Mark Twain **D.** Stephen King

3. What is the lowest-lying capital city in the world?

   A. Amman **B.** Amsterdam

   C. Baku **D.** Tehran

4. What did Travis Scott and Kylie Jenner name their baby?

   A. Raini **B.** Stormi

   C. Sunni **D.** Windi

5. Who, as of 2021, is the youngest winner of a Nobel Prize?

   A. Marie Curie **B.** Albert Einstein

   C. Greta Thunberg **D.** Malala Yousafzai

6. Tequila is named after what?

   A. A dance **B.** An insect

   C. A cactus **D.** A town

Go to page 208 for the answers.

Who or what comes next in each of these sequences?

1. $\dfrac{S}{1}, \dfrac{M}{2}, \dfrac{C}{4}, \dfrac{Q}{8}, \dfrac{S}{16} \ldots$?
2. Gretl, Marta, Brigitta, Kurt . . .?
3. Waterloo, Hungerford, Westminster, Lambeth . . .?
4. Lenin, Stalin, Khrushchev, Brezhnev . . .?
5. Epic shops, scarce yips, spacey bib, posy triceps . . .?

The answers are on page 204.

The answers are on page 204.

♔ DISNEY AND PIXAR

These questions all relate to Disney and Pixar movies. How many can you answer?

1. Which Pixar character comes from the Gamma Quadrant of Sector 4?
2. What was the sequel to *101 Dalmatians*?
3. In *Inside Out*, Riley's five emotions personified by characters are Joy, Fear, Disgust, Anger and what?
4. Which was the first full-length Disney animation?
5. What is unusual about the Parr family, who feature in a 2004 Pixar film?
6. Which Pixar character suffers from anterograde amnesia?
7. Which Disney film is based on *The Snow Queen* by Hans Christian Andersen?
8. Who was Bambi's rabbit friend?
9. Which Disney film is set in Tsenacommacah?
10. In which Pixar film does Sigourney Weaver play a computer?

Turn to page 199 for the answers.

Can you match the fandoms to the objects of their appreciation? (For a harder game, and more points, play 'blind' without the answers in the second grid.)

1. Katy Kats	2. Pine Nuts	3. Sheerios	4. Mixers
5. Gould Diggers	6. Beliebers	7. Achievers	8. Cumber-bitches
9. Dunderheads	10. Peabodies	11. Wayniacs	12. Victims

A. *The Office* (US)	B. Benedict Cumberbatch	C. Black Eyed Peas	D. *The Big Lebowski*
E. Lil' Wayne	F. Chris Pine	G. Little Mix	H. The Killers
I. Ellie Goulding	J. Katy Perry	K. Ed Sheeran	L. Justin Bieber

Find the solution on page 195.

The clues correspond to single letters. The letters make a coiled-up, 9-letter word. The word can start in any square, and can run in any direction, but always through adjacent squares. Solve the clues to unscramble the word.

Clue: A shade of green.

Middle initial of Grant and Truman	Online UK newspaper	Rho
Surname of B. A. Baracus actor	Individual player in Baltimore baseball team	*Claudius*
SI unit of electrical current	Ascorbic acid vitamin	Ian Watkins of Steps

The answers are on page 192.

Try to answer these fifty-fifty questions.

1. A pickle is the collective word for which animal, **raccoons** or **sea cucumbers**?

2. In *Romeo and Juliet*, which family was Juliet, **Montague** or **Capulet**?

3. Which is older, **Triassic** or **Jurassic**?

4. Which is larger in area, **Brazil** or **Australia**?

5. Whose real name is Robyn Fenty, **Rihanna** or **Ariana Grande**?

The answers are on page 216.

Try to answer these miscellaneous questions.

1. What links Karen Carpenter, Dave Grohl and Phil Collins?
2. What animal appears in the Alfa Romeo logo?
3. Which English King died in 1066 and was succeeded by Harold?
4. Which author described their trilogy, the bestselling novels of 2012, as 'my midlife crisis writ large'?
5. What is measured by the Scoville scale?
6. The acronym HOMES is used to help remember which geographical feature of North America?
7. Diacetylmorphine is more commonly known as what?
8. Who did artist Cornelia Parker put in a glass case for an installation called 'The Maybe'?
9. South onto revealing an old burial site? (anag, 6,3)
10. Which British boxer, who was WBC, WBA and IBF heavyweight champion, had a cameo role in the movie *Ocean's 11*?
11. What are Palatine, Capitoline, Quirinal, Viminal, Esquiline, Caelian and Aventine collectively known as?
12. Easter Island is a territory of which country?
13. Dendrochronology is the practice of what?
14. In Portuguese 'dedos dos pés' – literally 'feet fingers' – means what in English?
15. Which book begins with a character celebrating his eleventy-first birthday?

Answers on page 188.

Arrange the items in each of these lists in the correct order.

1. Starting with the smallest, arrange these human bones in order of size.

    - Clavicle
    - Metatarsal
    - Ulna
    - Femur
    - Stapes

2. Starting with the earliest, put these holidays in order of when they appear on the annual calendar.

    - May Day
    - St David's Day
    - Thanksgiving (US)
    - Labor Day (US)
    - St Patrick's Day

3. Starting with the fewest, arrange these artists according to how many UK number ones they have had.

    - The Beatles
    - Spice Girls
    - Tinie Tempah
    - Madonna
    - Take That

4. Starting with the earliest, in what order did these athletes win their first Olympic gold medal?

    - Cathy Freeman
    - Nadia Comăneci
    - Usain Bolt
    - Mark Spitz
    - Michael Johnson

Go to page 196 for the answers.

Which of these is more, which is less . . . or are they the same?

1. Which has more physical land borders with other countries, **Denmark** or **Portugal**? Or are they the same?
2. Which are there more of, **Beatrix Potter Tales** or **Famous Five stories** (by Enid Blyton)? Or are they the same?
3. Which are there more of, **gallons in a bushel** or **pints in a gallon**? Or are they the same?
4. Which are there more of, **US states bordering no other states** or **US states bordering one other state**? Or are they the same?
5. Who was older (in years) when they died, **Alexander the Great** or **Ayrton Senna**? Or were they the same?

Answers on page 216.

👑 MONEY

These questions all relate to money. How many can you answer?

1. Which currency, in 1704, was set equal to 100 kopeks, making it the world's first decimal currency?
2. What eponymous gold coin was first introduced by Henry VII?
3. Who chartered the First Bank of the United States in 1791?
4. What is Hong Kong's share index called?
5. Cops examine laundered a national currency? (anag. 7,4)
6. Which trader brought down Barings Bank?
7. CHF is the abbreviation for the currency of which country?
8. The Spanish dollar is regarded as the first international currency. How many reales were in a Spanish dollar?
9. What is a group of producers who collaborate to set prices?
10. Cardano, Polkadot and Tether are examples of what type of currency?

The answers are on page 208.

Try to pick the correct option for each of these questions.

1. A bloat is the collective term for which animal?
   - **A.** Hippopotamus
   - **B.** Jellyfish
   - **C.** Pufferfish
   - **D.** Sloth

2. In rugby union, backs are the leading points scorers, but who has scored the most points for England playing as a forward (as of 2021)?
   - **A.** Neil Back
   - **B.** Lawrence Dallaglio
   - **C.** Richard Hill
   - **D.** Billy Vunipola

3. 'She say, "Do you love me?" I tell her, "Only partly"' . . . Who sang these words?
   - **A.** Drake
   - **B.** Chance
   - **C.** DJ Khaled
   - **D.** Major Lazer

4. Who wrote *Mary Poppins*?
   - **A.** E. Nesbit
   - **B.** J. M. Barrie
   - **C.** P. L. Travers
   - **D.** T. H. White

5. In 2019 Chris Pratt wed the daughter of a former Hollywood tough guy actor. Who?
   - **A.** Katherine Schwarzenegger
   - **B.** Sophia Rose Stallone
   - **C.** Bianca Van Damme
   - **D.** Scout Willis

6. Which is the closest US state to Africa?
   - **A.** Maine
   - **B.** Massachusetts
   - **C.** North Carolina
   - **D.** Florida

Answers on page 212.

THE WISDOM OF THE CROWD: YEARS TO REACH THE MOON

The Ministry of Quizzes asked 200 people in the UK: '*How many years elapsed between the Wright Brothers' first powered flight and Neil Armstrong setting foot on the Moon?*' This is how they responded:

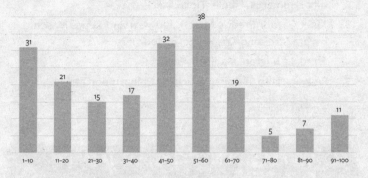

(For instance, 31 people gave an answer in the range of 1 and 10.*)

 The middle answer	48	 The most popular answer	50	 The average answer	43

60	50	60	52
The middle answer from people aged over 30	The middle answer from people aged 30 or under	The most popular answer from men	The most popular answer from women

Based on this data, or otherwise, what is *your* estimate of the number of years between the first powered flight and the first Moon landing?

The answer is on page 204.

* 4 people answered 'don't know'; their responses have not been included.

👑 WHAT COMES NEXT? II

Who or what comes next in each of these sequences?

1. Prince Albert of Saxe-Coburg, Alexandra of Denmark, Mary of Teck, Elizabeth Bowes-Lyon of Scotland . . .?

2. Ulna, Humerus, Fibula, Tibia . . .?

3. Janet Gaynor/Fredric March, Judy Garland/James Mason, Barbra Streisand/Kris Kristofferson . . .?

4. Third, Lexington, Madison, Park . . .?

5. Re-knit, rialto, old sire, solari, Mr China, moon rap . . .?

See page 199 for the answers.

👑 US PRESIDENTS CALLED JAMES OR JOHN

Try to list the **10** US presidents named James or John. Earn points for more obscure answers, lose points for incorrect answers.

Go to page 195 for the answers.

👑 IN COMMON II

What do the terms in each of these lists have in common?

1. High, take, Saturn, Famous, Babylon.
2. Monaco, Djibouti, Luxembourg, Singapore.
3. Tibetan, rhombus, campsite, audiotape, toxic.
4. Herm, Jethou, Brecqhou, Sark.
5. House, Chapel, Hotel, Jailhouse.

See page 188 for the answers.

Find each answer using the clues in turn – the least number of clues the better.

1. What is this?

    - It is around 15 centimetres long, and an elongated S-shape.
    - Its name in Latin means 'little key' because it can rotate around its long axis.
    - It is the most commonly broken bone in the human body.
    - It has been nicknamed 'the beauty bone'.

2. Who is this?

    - The only woman he loved left him on Christmas Day.
    - He has been played by Alastair Sim (1951), Michael Caine (1992) and Patrick Stewart (1999).
    - His story was first published on 19 December 1843 and was sold out by Christmas Eve.
    - His dead business partner, Jacob Marley, visits him as a ghost.

3. When (which year) is this?

    - *GoldenEye*, Pierce Brosnan's first outing as James Bond, has its premiere.
    - Oasis have a UK number one with 'Some Might Say' and Blur with 'Country House'.
    - South Africa win the Rugby World Cup for the first time.
    - Microsoft release Windows 95.

Find the answers on page 190.

Try to answer these miscellaneous questions.

1. What animal appears in the Abercrombie and Fitch logo?
2. What word goes after 'purple', 'eye' and 'cabbage'?
3. With which symbol are Edward IV of England and Louis XIV of France both associated?
4. The Carpathian Mountains are in which continent?
5. The Chinese word for which bird means 'eagle with a cat head'?
6. What social restriction, introduced in the UK by the Defence of the Realm Act of 1914, was not relaxed until 2005?
7. In what part of the human body are the talus, calcaneus, cuboid and navicular bones found?
8. In computing, what does the 'A' stand for in WAN, LAN or MAN?
9. What is the alter ego of Carol Danvers?
10. At which winter sports resort is the Cresta Run?
11. Who sometimes wrote under the pen name of Mary Westmacott?
12. What TV series is the story of Walter White, a school teacher who turns to criminal activity to fund medical treatment?
13. In Mexico it is the Rio Bravo, what is it called in the US?
14. What spirit goes into a Sazerac, a Manhattan and an Old Fashioned?
15. Why are Big Diomede Island and Little Diomede Island, which are 2.5 miles apart, known colloquially as Tomorrow Island and Yesterday Island?

See page 184 for the answers.

The clues in the grid correspond to numbers. The rows, columns and the two diagonals add up to the same number – the Magic Number. Use the clues to find this Magic Number and solve the grid!

Clue to the Magic Number: The smallest number with exactly ten divisors.

Lowest number that can't be scored with a single dart	Time zones across the 50 US states	Red balls in snooker	Ghosts in Pac-Man
People in Noah's Ark	'Legs'	2^4	Atomic number of aluminium
Circles of Hell	Bravo	Uno	Minimum age to be President of France
Sides on a STOP sign	Sides on a hendecagon	Feathers in a standard shuttlecock	Countries in South America

Go to page 220 for the solution.

Try to answer these fifty-fifty questions.

1. In the American Civil War, what colour was the Confederate uniform, **Blue** or **Grey**?

2. Which is further north, the **Shetland Islands** or the **Orkney Islands**?

3. 'Cause I got that boom boom that all the boys chase.' What song does this line come from? '**All About That Bass**' by Meghan Trainor or '**Juice**' by Lizzo?

4. Which is longer, the **small intestine** or the **large intestine**?

5. Which official presides over a game of netball, a **referee** or an **umpire**?

The answers are on page 184.

👑 CONNECTIONS 14

The answers to these questions share a link . . . what is it?

1. Which root vegetable, *Helianthus tuberosus*, has a capital city in its common name and is also known as 'sunroot' and 'earth apple'?

2. What was the conflict between England and France that included the battles of Crécy, Poitiers and Agincourt?

3. What headwear is sported by the Man from Del Monte?

4. Built in Paris in 1604, and having a double span connecting the Île de la Cité to the left and right banks of the Seine, what does 'Pont Neuf' mean in English?

5. In which game do players have the objective of moving pieces across a board divided into hexagonal spaces, using single step moves or moves that jump over other pieces?

What connection do these answers share?

Find out if you are right on page 200.

Try to pick the correct option for each of these questions.

1. Travelling due south from the centre of Detroit in the US, what is the next country you would hit?

    A. Canada   **B.** Cuba

    C. Mexico   **D.** Panama

2. How long does a perennial plant live for?

    A. Less than one year   **B.** One year

    C. Two years   **D.** More than two years

3. H5N1 is alternatively known as what?

    A. Avian Flu   **B.** COVID

    C. SARS   **D.** Spanish Flu

4. Mr Jinx is a devious cat in which film?

    A. *Cheaper by the Dozen*   **B.** *Daddy's Home*

    C. *Home Alone*   **D.** *Meet the Parents*

5. Which book, a translation of a literary classic entirely into emojis, was added to the US Library of Congress in 2013?

    A. *Emoji in the Rye*   **B.** *Emoji Dick*

    C. *Gone with the Emoji*   **D.** *Emoji-22*

6. 'Tethered jumping', the inspiration for the modern sport of bungee jumping, is a historic rite of passage for young men in which country?

    A. Cameroon   **B.** Equatorial Guinea

    C. Papua New Guinea   **D.** Vanuatu

Go to page 208 for the answers.

Work out the links between the answers to the questions to solve the grid. Use the grid to help you answer all the questions.

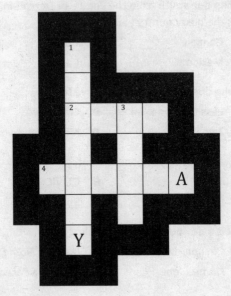

2 Across (4 letters)

1. What can be the spar at the foot of the mainsail of a yacht or a pole that a microphone attaches to?

2. Which of the Mr Men is afraid of everything?

3. Which surname is shared by the 41st and 43rd presidents of the United States?

4. What is the common name for around 80 species of reptile belonging to the genus *Varanus*, noted for their large size, long necks and powerful tails and claws?

5. 'Leonids' and 'Perseids' are examples of what type of celestial phenomenon?

. . . what is the link?

4 Across (6)

1. 'To boldly go' is an example of what, often maligned, grammatical construction?
2. What system of government in Rome lasted from 509 BC to 27 BC, ending with the establishment of the Roman Empire?
3. What part of a mammal consists of epidermis and dermis?
4. 'Lavash', 'Rugbrød' and 'Pistolet' are types of what staple food?
5. What word goes with 'asteroid', 'rust' and 'safety'?

. . . what is the link?

1 Down (7)

1. What does the 'B' stand for in the acronym ISBN?
2. Virus yet in chaotic academic institution (anag, 10)?
3. Which is the only country in the world to be entirely designated as a World Heritage Site?
4. What is a kinetic sculpture, suspended in mid-air with balanced parts set in motion by air currents?
5. What did referees have for the first time at the 1970 World Cup in Mexico?

. . . what is the link?

3 Down (4)

1. The *Salticidae* group of spiders do not spin webs, but are named after what athletic physical ability they instead use to catch prey?
2. In the UK, what title is taken by doctors who gain membership of the Royal College of Surgeons?
3. Which controversial Ford model was the subject of a mass recall in 1978 due to its propensity to catch fire on rear collision?
4. Which watery area of the UK became a National Park in 1988?
5. In medicine, renal refers to which organ of the body?

. . . what is the link?

Find the solution on page 203.

Try to answer these miscellaneous questions.

1. Who is the only actor to have appeared in all nine *Star Wars* films?

2. 'Magdalena', 'smorgastarta', and 'eerschecke' are types of what?

3. Alaska, Texas and California are the three largest states in the US, what is the fourth?

4. What word links 'forest', 'place' and 'station'?

5. Which 1959 film had working titles of 'Breathless' and 'The Man in Lincoln's Nose'?

6. Which twentieth-century British Prime Minister spoke English as a second language?

7. Whose novels include *The Blind Assassin*, *The Testaments* and *The Handmaid's Tale*?

8. Vassily Smyslov, Tigran Petrosian and Anatoly Karpov have all been world champions in what?

9. Chris Ofili, the Turner Prize-winning artist, is known for incorporating what substance into his paintings?

10. Damsons, greengages and mirabelles are variants of which fruit?

11. Which military leader had a horse called Marengo?

12. The Major Oak, a British tree thought to be 1,000 years old, is in which forest?

13. Two chemical elements begin with 'Z', Zirconium is one, what is the other?

14. Who wrote the music for *Billy Elliot*?

15. Soft towel spread out at British seaside resort? (anag, 9)

Answers on page 195.

👑 LARGE COUNTRIES

Try to list the **10** largest countries in the world by area. Earn points for more obscure answers, lose points for incorrect answers.

See page 192 for the answers.

👑 ODD ONE OUT 10

Which is the odd one out in each of these lists, and why?

1. Tiger, Bear, Whale, Basking.
2. Houston, Lexington, Madison, Park.
3. Michael Palin, Graham Chapman, Terry Gilliam, Douglas Adams.
4. *Madame Butterfly, Tosca, La Bohème, La Traviata.*
5. New York Jets, Chicago Bears, San Francisco Giants, Kansas City Chiefs.

The answers are on page 188.

👑 WHAT COMES NEXT? 12

Who or what comes next in each of these sequences?

1. King Juan Carlos I, Bill Clinton, William Deane, Konstantinos Stephanopoulos, Hu Jintao . . .?
2. Ganymede, Titan, Callisto, Io . . .?
3. Cecil Parker, Peter Sellers, Danny Green, Herbert Lom . . .?
4. Grand piano, reed and pipe organ, glockenspiel, bass guitar, double-speed guitar, two slightly distorted guitars, Spanish guitar and acoustic guitar . . .?
5. Virginia, Washington, West Virginia, Wisconsin . . .?

Go to page 184 for the answers.

Find each answer using the clues in turn – the least number of clues the better.

1. When (which year) is this?
   - Pixar Animation Studios is founded, with funding from Steve Jobs.
   - Halley's Comet becomes visible from Earth with the naked eye, reaching the nearest point of its orbit to the sun.
   - The nuclear power plant at Chernobyl explodes.
   - Argentina wins the World Cup, beating Germany 3–2 in the Estadio Azteca in Mexico City.

2. Where is this?
   - The largest city in a region known as the 'Golden Horseshoe', named for its economic prosperity.
   - Served by Pearson Airport, the country's busiest airport, with around 50 million passengers per year.
   - Home of a sports franchise called the Blue Jays.
   - The most populous city in Canada.

3. Who is this?
   - He was deported from Germany in 1960 for breaking immigration rules for working when under the age of 18.
   - He played Mr Papadopolous in *Monty Python's Life of Brian*.
   - He died in 2001 and, in accordance with his wishes, his ashes were taken to India and scattered over the River Ganges.
   - He was the first member of The Beatles to have a solo number one.

See page 219 for the answers.

Try to pick the correct option for each of these questions.

1. What is the first thing eaten by *The Very Hungry Caterpillar*?
    - **A.** Apple
    - **B.** Pear
    - **C.** Salami
    - **D.** Strawberry

2. Status Quo opened the bill at Live Aid with 'Rockin' All Over the World', but which act followed them?
    - **A.** The Boomtown Rats
    - **B.** Nik Kershaw
    - **C.** The Style Council
    - **D.** Ultravox

3. In which country is the city in the world that regularly receives the greatest annual snowfall?
    - **A.** Canada
    - **B.** Japan
    - **C.** Switzerland
    - **D.** The United States

4. Which modern dating term describes a person's state of ambivalence where they don't want to end but neither want to actively pursue their relationship?
    - **A.** Ghosting
    - **B.** Benching
    - **C.** Orbiting
    - **D.** Kittenfishing

5. Which chemical element has a name deriving from the German word for 'goblin'?
    - **A.** Copper
    - **B.** Cobalt
    - **C.** Gold
    - **D.** Iron

6. Which is the oldest international sporting trophy?
    - **A.** The Americas Cup
    - **B.** The Ashes
    - **C.** The Calcutta Cup
    - **D.** The Davis Cup

See page 216 for the answers.

These questions refer to US states, pictured in outline form. Some questions may give you clues to the answers to others. Use this – and your knowledge, of course – to work out as many of their identities as you can . . . and answer the question. Note that they are all oriented with north at the top, but are not necessarily to the same scale.

1. Which *three* have coastlines on the Pacific?

2. Which *two* share a border with Mexico?

3. Which takes its name from the river on its eastern border?

4. Which *two* begin with W?

5. Which *four* share borders with Canada?

6. Which *two* have coastlines on the Atlantic?

7. Which has the smallest population, and a state capital of Cheyenne?

8. Which *three* begin with M?

9. Which *two* share their names with their largest city?

10. Which is home to the ski resorts of Boulder, Aspen and Vail, and is also the squarest state?

11. Which is the Bluegrass State, and the most associated with horse racing?

12. Which *three* have coastlines on the Gulf of Mexico?

13. Which begins with P?

14. Which *two* are in the Mountain time zone?

15. Which is home to Las Vegas and Area 51?

16. Which *two* have 12 or more letters in their names?

Find the solution on page 212.

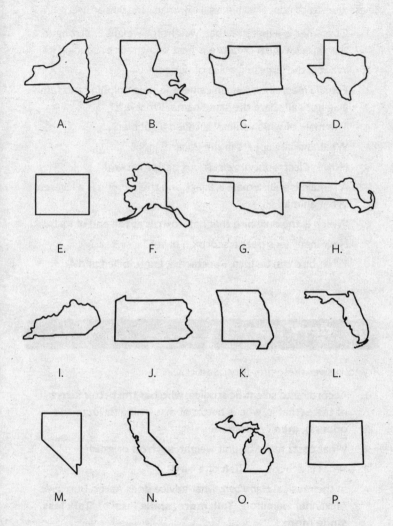

A.

B.

C.

D.

E.

F.

G.

H.

I.

J.

K.

L.

M.

N.

O.

P.

165

👑 THE ANIMAL KINGDOM

These questions concern animals. How many can you answer?

1. Gossamer is a material that, weight for weight, is stronger than steel. Which creature is best known for producing it?

2. What is the largest species of penguin?

3. Female elephants, female camels, female dolphins and female alligators all share the same name. What is it?

4. The male of which animal is called a gobbler?

5. What animal appears in the Bacardi logo?

6. How is *Electrophorus electricus* better known?

7. A female is a jill, a male is a jack and their young is a leveret. What animal?

8. Which is the only bird that has nostrils at the end of its beak?

9. How many legs does a scorpion have?

10. What bird can be Inca, Spectacled, Large-billed and Arctic?

The answers are on page 208.

👑 FIFTY-FIFTY 15

Try to answer these fifty-fifty questions.

1. According to scientific studies, who has the better sense of taste (that is, who is better at discerning flavours and odours), **men** or **women**?

2. What costs more by unit weight, **saffron** or **gold**?

3. What is a 'booby', a **fish** or a **bird**?

4. In the musical *Hamilton*, what advice does Aaron Burr give Alexander Hamilton, '**Talk more, smile less**' or '**Talk less, smile more**'?

5. What was found in the Zhoukoudian Cave, **Peking Man** or the **Terracotta Army**?

See page 203 for the answers.

Try to answer these miscellaneous questions.

1. What number is 'clickety-click' in bingo?
2. Which battle, fought in Somerset in 1685, is regarded as the last battle fought on English soil?
3. Which is the only country that borders both Iraq and Iran?
4. How many strings does a ukulele have?
5. Edward John Smith is known to history for captaining which vessel?
6. What animal lives in a drey?
7. What food group is cut out under the Atkins Diet?
8. It was originally called 'Bolshaya Gora', then 'Densmore's Mountain' and today it is called 'Denali'. How is it still more popularly known?
9. What is the singular of plural word 'genera'?
10. The football team Espanyol play in which Spanish city?
11. Which detective created by Edith Pargeter investigated murders in twelfth-century England?
12. Who did Flora MacDonald help escape to Skye disguised as her maid?
13. Nephology is a branch of meteorology, studying what?
14. Mombasa is a port in which country?
15. What is the first name of Professor McGonagall in the Harry Potter books?

Go to page 199 for the answers.

Which is the odd one out in each of these lists, and why?

1. Gooseberry, Banana, Cherry, Blueberry.
2. Commander, Colonel, Major, General.
3. C sharp, D sharp, E sharp, F sharp, B flat.
4. Ronald Reagan, George H. W. Bush, Bill Clinton, George W. Bush, Barack Obama.
5. 'Call me Ishmael', 'Marley was dead to begin with', 'After all, tomorrow is another day', 'It was a bright cold day in April and the clocks were striking thirteen', 'Last night I dreamt I went to Manderley again'.

Go to page 192 for the answers.

👑 IN COMMON 12

What do the terms in each of these lists have in common?

1. Cable, Perch, Peck, Drachm, Slug.
2. Farewell, Fear, Cod, Cornwall, Trafalgar.
3. Love, Peace, Plenty, Truth.
4. 'A former child star torments her paraplegic sister in their decaying Hollywood mansion' (1962), 'A couple's attitudes are challenged when their daughter introduces them to her African American fiancé' (1967), 'Two potheads wake up after a night of partying and cannot remember where they parked their car' (2000), 'A toon-hating detective is a cartoon rabbit's only hope to prove his innocence when he is accused of murder' (1988).
5. Eton, Norfolk, donkey, Eisenhower, bomber.

Answers on page 195.

👑 MATCHING PAIRS: ANIMALS AND THEIR LATIN NAMES

Can you match the Latin names to the animals? (For a harder game, and more points, play 'blind' without the answers in the second grid.)

1. Canis lupus familiaris	2. Thunnus thynnus	3. Panthera leo	4. Felis catus
5. Pan troglodytes	6. Equus ferus caballus	7. Panthera pardus	8. Ursus americanus
9. Vulpes vulpes	10. Carcharodon carcharias	11. Orcinus orca	12. Castor canadensis

A. Chimpanzee	B. Black bear	C. Domestic dog	D. Atlantic bluefin tuna
E. Great white shark	F. Red fox	G. Lion	H. Killer whale
I. Leopard	J. Beaver	K. Domestic cat	L. Horse

Turn to page 208 for the solution.

The clues in the grid relate to the numbers 1 to 9. No number is repeated. Use a process of elimination to work out which number is which.

Funnels on the *Titanic*	Countries with nuclear weapons	Number of arms Nelson had in 1796
Points for the letter 'J' in Scrabble	три	Stages of grief
Geese a-laying	Names in the chorus of 'Mambo No. 5'	Atomic number of hydrogen

Go to page 184 to see the solution.

The answers to these questions share a link . . . can you work out what it is?

1.   What mathematical method for studying continuous change was developed independently in the late seventeenth century by Isaac Newton and Gottfried Wilhelm Leibniz?
2.   What word goes with 'sugar', 'tomato' and 'duff'?
3.   Which vegetable, often eaten at Christmas, is the edible buds of *Brassica oleracea* of the Gemmifera Group of cabbages?
4.   Which movie character has been played by Corey Carrier, Sean Patrick Flanery, River Phoenix and Harrison Ford?
5.   What colour is the Chicago River dyed each year on 17 March?

What connection do these answers share?

Find out if you are right on page 219.

👑 FAMOUS PAINTINGS

Try to list the **10** most famous paintings in the world (according to worldatlas.com). Earn points for more obscure answers, lose points for incorrect answers.

Go to page 216 for the answers.

👑 CHINA

These questions are all about China. How many can you answer?

1. What is notable about the Qin and Qing dynasties?
2. What was the nickname of China's Olympic stadium in Beijing?
3. What two-word name for a style of Chinese food, served as a starter or a light snack, means 'touches the heart'?
4. The name of which Chinese city means 'fragrant harbour'?
5. 'Cha dao' is the art of making what?
6. In Venice it is 2.4 miles long. In China it is 1,104 miles in length. What?
7. What 2004 thriller with a Chinese-related title starred Denzel Washington, Meryl Streep and Jon Voight?
8. Li Na is associated with which sport?
9. The Chinese word 'Jinrikisha' means literally 'human-powered vehicle'. What is it called in English?
10. Traditionally, what colour does a bride wear at a Chinese wedding?

Answers on page 212.

Find each answer using the clues in turn – the least number of clues the better.

1. What is this?
    - It was named after a 1973 novel by J. P. Donleavy about the return of an Irish American man to New York from Ireland.
    - It was recorded at Abbey Road studios in London in March 1987.
    - It contains the line 'Got on a lucky one, came in eighteen-to-one'.
    - On an ITV poll in December 2012, it was voted 'The Nation's Favourite Christmas Song'.

2. Where is this?
    - As of 2021 it is the fifth most populous country in the world.
    - It is a nuclear power.
    - The Indus Valley, which gave rise to one of the first major civilizations, is located here.
    - It is home to the Karakorum Highway, the world's highest paved road, and K2, the world's second-highest mountain.

3. When (which year) is this?
    - Kosovo declares independence from Serbia.
    - Spotify launches its music streaming service in Sweden.
    - Lehman Brothers bank files for bankruptcy.
    - Barack Obama is elected the 44th President of the United States.

See page 188 for the answers.

The Ministry of Quizzes translated distinctive lines from three well-known karaoke classics . . . into Esperanto. Can you recognize them? (The titles of the songs are in brackets, below each).

♫ **1.**

'Kaj tiel Sally povas atendi
Ŝi scias, ke estas tro malfrue'
('Ne Rigardu Malantaŭen en Kolero')

♫ **2.**

'Jes, mi estas nur adoleska malpuraĵo, bebo
Aŭskultu Iron Maiden eble kun mi'
('Adoleska Malpuraĵo')

♫ **3.**

'Kiel virgulino
Tuŝita por la unua fojo'
('Kiel Virgulino')

♫ **4.**

'Mi ricevis la okulon de la tigro
Batalanto
Dancante tra la fajro'
('Muĝi')

♫ **5.**

'Kaj mi pensas, ke estos longa tempo'
('Raketa Viro')

Find the answers on page 203.

Arrange the items in each of these lists in the correct order.

1. Starting with the earliest, put these cities in order of when they first hosted the Summer Olympics.
    - Barcelona
    - Mexico City
    - Seoul
    - Beijing
    - Rome

2. Starting with the slowest, put these animals in order of how fast they can run or swim.
    - Cheetah
    - Rabbit
    - Swordfish
    - Ostrich
    - Roadrunner

3. Starting with the earliest, put these events in history in order of when they occurred.
    - Alexander defeats Darius III
    - Building of the Great Pyramid at Giza
    - First Olympiad in Greece
    - Birth of Mohammad
    - Death of Julius Caesar

4. Going from west to east, arrange these stations on the Central Line of the London Underground.
    - Bank
    - Oxford Circus
    - Stratford
    - Notting Hill Gate
    - Shepherd's Bush

The answers are on page 204.

Try to pick the correct option for each of these questions.

1. Which rock duo started out as Tom and Jerry?

    A. The Everly Brothers   **B.** Hall and Oates

    C. The Righteous Brothers **D.** Simon and Garfunkel

2. Which adult animal has the most teeth?

    A. Elephant   **B.** Lion

    C. Panda   **D.** Sloth

3. Which place in the UK has a station called 'Shrub Hill'?

    A. Chester   **B.** Gloucester

    C. Kidderminster   **D.** Worcester

4. Mount Kosciuszko is in which country?

    A. Australia   **B.** Georgia

    C. Poland   **D.** Russia

5. Kim Kardashian and Kanye West had a daughter in 2013.
    What did they name her?

    A. North   **B.** South

    C. East   **D.** West

6. Which Olympic Games was opened by the Duke of
    Edinburgh?

    A. London, 1948   **B.** Melbourne, 1956

    C. Montreal, 1976   **D.** London, 2012

Answers on page 188.

Which of these is more, which is less . . . or are they the same?

1. Which is greater, the number of bones (cervical vertebrae) in the **neck of a human** or the **neck of a giraffe**? Or are they the same?

2. Which are there more of, chemical **elements with 5-letter names**, or **elements with 4-letter names**? Or are they the same?

3. Which number is greater, **CMI** or **999**? Or are they the same?

4. Who was older when they died, **John F. Kennedy** or **Julius Caesar**? Or were they the same age?

5. Which are there more of, different types of instruments in the **woodwind section** or **brass section** of a standard orchestra? Or are they the same?

Answers on page 223.

👑 FIFTY-FIFTY 16

Try to answer these fifty-fifty questions.

1. What term applies to a group of fish swimming in the same direction or in a coordinated fashion, a **school** or a **shoal**?

2. Which river is longer, the **Mississippi** or the **Missouri**?

3. Where in the human body are the metacarpals, in the **hand** or the **foot**?

4. Which part of the city did the Berlin Wall encircle, **East Berlin** or **West Berlin**?

5. Which ascends from the floor, a **stalactite** or a **stalagmite**?

See page 219 for the answers.

The clues in the grid correspond to numbers. The rows, columns and the two diagonals add up to the same number – the Magic Number. Use the clues to find this Magic Number and solve the grid!

Clue to the Magic Number: Long playing record.

Novels by Oscar Wilde	Age in the UK at which it becomes your responsibility to wear a seatbelt	Pounds in a stone	US states beginning with 'A'
Weeks 'Despacito' was number one in the UK	Books in the Harry Potter series	Pussycat Dolls	Oscars won by *The English Patient*
Points for the letter 'X' in Scrabble	Hurdles jumped by each athlete in the women's 100m hurdles	X	Pillars of Islam
+☰	'One Little Duck'	Primary colours	Members of the United Nations Security Council

Go to page 215 for the solution.

Try to answer these miscellaneous questions.

1. Who has a pet called Mr Bigglesworth?
2. At which Olympics did Kelly Holmes win her two gold medals?
3. Which river is Minneapolis on?
4. The Welsh prefix 'caer' found in Caernarfon and Caerphilly means what?
5. What classic 1952 western starring Gary Cooper and Grace Kelly was nominated for seven Academy Awards?
6. In the Highway Code, only one triangular warning sign has colours other than red, black and white. What is it warning of?
7. What children's song ends with the line 'life is but a dream'?
8. What do the lacrimal glands produce?
9. If a fjord is a flooded glacial valley, what is a ria?
10. Who in her autobiography described her husband as a 'unicorn', 'unusual to the point of seeming almost unreal'?
11. What is pumpernickel a type of?
12. What was the first comic book film to be nominated for Best Picture Oscar?
13. In which UK town is the Turner Contemporary art gallery?
14. Which city in Louisiana is named after a French aristocrat and military leader?
15. What craft, launched in 1957, had a name which in its local language means 'fellow traveller'?

Go to page 212 for the answers.

Can you match these characters to the novels they appear in? (For a harder game, and more points, play 'blind' without the answers in the second grid.)

1. Jack Torrance	2. Bathsheba Everdene	3. Natasha Rostova	4. Becky Sharp
5. Dorothea Brooke	6. Ignatius J. Reilly	7. Daniel Cleaver	8. Agatha Trunchbull
9. Aibileen Clark	10. Fanny Price	11. Tonya Gromeko	12. Maxim de Winter

A. *The Help*	B. *Middlemarch*	C. *The Shining*	D. *Matilda*
E. *Doctor Zhivago*	F. *Mansfield Park*	G. *War and Peace*	H. *Far from the Madding Crowd*
I. *Rebecca*	J. *A Confederacy of Dunces*	K. *Bridget Jones's Diary*	L. *Vanity Fair*

Turn to page 208 for the solution.

Find each answer using the clues in turn – the least number of clues the better.

1. **Where is this?**
   - The games of poker and craps are thought to have originated here in the 1820s.
   - The motto of this city is *'laissez les bon temps rouler'* ('let the good times roll').
   - It is famous for an annual celebration, where people wear green, purple and gold.
   - It is named after the Duke of Orleans, and goes by the nickname of 'The Big Easy'.

2. **Who is this?**
   - Her first name is from India and means 'lotus'.
   - Her motto (which comes from her mother) is, 'You may be the first, but make sure you're not the last'.
   - Her supporters are known as the 'KHive'.
   - She was the first female, and the first African American, and the first Asian American vice president in US history.

3. **When (which year) is this?**
   - The last ever videocassette recorder is manufactured.
   - The Panama Papers, confidential documents containing details of offshore investments of noted personalities, politicians and heads of state, are leaked.
   - The United Kingdom votes in a referendum to leave the European Union.
   - Rio de Janeiro hosts the Summer Olympic Games.

See page 203 for the answers.

Which is the odd one out in each of these lists, and why?

1. Gypsy, Swallowtail, Red Admiral, Painted Lady.
2. London, Southwark, Millennium, Westminster, Lambeth.
3. Henry VI, Henry VII, Henry VIII, Edward VI.
4. Vermeer, Caravaggio, Pieter Bruegel the Elder, Rembrandt.
5. Agoraphobia, Arachnophobia, Murophobia, Ophidiophobia, Ornithophobia.

See page 195 for the answers.

👑 LAST WORDS

These questions concern last words. How many can you answer?

1. Which writer's last words were reputedly 'Either that wallpaper goes – or I do'?
2. 'Just give me a kiss, like this' is the last line of which song?
3. Which poem ends with 'And the mome raths outgrabe'?
4. Dylan Thomas's last words were: 'I've had eighteen straight _____, I think that's the record.' What did he have?
5. 'I know now why you cry. But it's something I can never do. Goodbye.' Which actor delivered this cyborg's final words?
6. Which song ends with the words 'I don't belong here'?
7. Which Roman emperor's final words were reputedly '*Qualis artifex pereo*' – 'What an artist dies in me!'
8. 'And, which is more, you'll be a man, my son' is the last line of which poem?
9. Which novel ends with: 'So we beat on, boats against the current, borne back ceaselessly into the past'?
10. 'Well, I'm back' is the last line of a well-known book and film. Which character says it?

Find the answers on page 184.

ANSWERS

1. Oscar Wilde; 2. 'Walk This Way' (Aerosmith/Run-DMC); 3. 'Jabberwocky' (Lewis Carroll); 4. Whiskies; 5. Arnold Schwarzenegger; 6. 'Creep' (Radiohead); 7. Nero; 8. 'If' (Rudyard Kipling); 9. *The Great Gatsby* (F. Scott Fitzgerald); 10. Samwise Gamgee (*The Lord of the Rings*).

2 points for each correct answer.

4	9$_a$	2$_b$
8	3$_c$	5$_d$
6	7$_e$	1

Notes:
a. US, UK, Russia, France, China, India, Pakistan, Israel and North Korea.
b. Nelson lost most of his right arm in 1797 in the attempt to capture Santa Cruz de Tenerife.
c. Russian word for three, pronounced 'tree'.
d. Denial, anger, bargaining, depression, acceptance.
e. Monica, Erica, Rita, Tina, Sandra, Mary, Jessica.

2 points for each correct answer.

1. Queen Elizabeth II (people opening the Summer Olympic Games, from 1992 forward . . . Barcelona, Atlanta, Sydney, Athens, Beijing, London); 2. The Moon (satellites in the solar system in decreasing order of size); 3. Alec Guinness (actors in *The Ladykillers* (1955) in order of when their characters expire); 4. Tubular bells (instruments named in the build-up to the end of Part I of Mike Oldfield's *Tubular Bells*); 5. Wyoming (last five US states in alphabetical order).

3 points for each correct answer.

1. Moose; 2. Patch; 3. The sun; 4. Europe (they stretch in an arc from the Czech Republic to Romania); 5. Owl; 6. Pub opening hours; 7. Foot; 8. Area (**W**ide **A**rea **N**etwork, **L**ocal **A**rea **N**etwork, **M**etropolitan **A**rea **N**etwork); 9. Captain Marvel; 10. St Moritz; 11. Agatha Christie; 12. *Breaking Bad*; 13. Rio Grande; 14. Whisky; 15. They are either side of the international date line (in the Bering Strait).

2 points for each correct answer.

1. Grey; 2. The Shetland Isles; 3. 'All About That Bass', Meghan Trainor; 4. The small intestine; 5. An umpire.

2 points for each correct answer.

1. Eye; 2. Kayak; 3. Ma'am; 4. Naan; 5. Rotavator.

The connection is **palindromes** – all read the same forwards and backwards.

2 points for each correct answer, 5 points for guessing the connection.

1. Brazil (countries in decreasing order of area); 2. Joaquin Phoenix (on-screen portrayals of the Joker, towards the present day); 3. 6 (single-digit numbers in alphabetical order); 4. Egypt (countries on the Nile, going towards the sea); 5. Cardinal

(ranks of the Catholic Church in order of seniority).

3 points for each correct answer.

THE WISDOM OF THE CROWD: TOP SPEED OF USAIN BOLT From page 124.

When he set the men's 100m world record in 2009 of 9.58s, Usain Bolt was travelling at **28** miles per hour.

The Ministry takes the middle answer (the median) to represent the Crowd's collective answer, in this case it was 27 . . . the Crowd was out by only one.

If you guessed 28, you beat the Crowd!

Award points for accuracy as follows:
A guess between 25 and 31, inclusive, 2 points
Or a guess between 27 and 29, inclusive, 5 points
Or a guess of 28, 10 points

ODD ONE OUT 8 From page 118.

1. Biscuit – the word 'dog' goes before this, it goes after all the others; 2. All are capital cities – Paris is the only one that is also the largest city in the country; 3. *Inception* – all the others have had sequels; 4. Trump – the others are names of airports (New York City, Washington D.C., Houston, Little Rock respectively); 5. The Queen of Hearts was not present at the mad tea party in *Alice in Wonderland*.

1 point for each correct answer, 2 bonus points for the correct reason.

ODDS AND ENDS 16 From page 110.

1. *Catch-22*; 2. Porcupine; 3. Gobi Desert; 4. Light; 5. 'That's All Folks'; 6. Phosphorus (P), hydrogen (H), oxygen (O), neon (Ne). It's possible to make it with three, replacing

hydrogen and oxygen with holmium (Ho); 7. Damascus (11,000 years); 8. Christmas; 9. Insomnia; 10. Chicago Bulls; 11. 'Someone Like You' (Adele); 12. Wind; 13. 1.5; 14. *Waiting for Godot*; 15. *The Royle Family*.

2 points for each correct answer.

IN COMMON 7 From page 100.

1. Names contain shipping forecast regions – Bailey, Fisher, Wight, Sole, Shannon; 2. Movies with 'last' – *The Last Emperor, The Last Jedi, Indiana Jones and the Last Crusade, Last Christmas*; 3. Dates of Apollo Moon landings; 4. Places in the titles of Shakespeare plays (*The Merry Wives of Windsor, The Merchant of Venice, Two Gentlemen of Verona, Timon of Athens*); 5. All become countries by adding an adjective (Equatorial Guinea, South Africa, North Macedonia, United Arab Emirates, East Timor).

3 points for each correct answer.

FOUR CLUES 6 From page 96.

1. The River Tweed
2. Oscar Wilde
3. 1992

Award 5 points for a correct answer from the first clue only, 3 points from the first two clues, 2 points from the first three, 1 point if all four clues were needed.

PUT IN ORDER 3 From page 47.

1. Israel (1), Panama (2), Australia (6), Brazil (27), United States (50)
2. Unicorn (1 horn), Bull (2), Triceratops (3), Jacob sheep (4), Hoplitomeryx (an extinct antelope-like creature, 5 horns)
3. Super Bowl (February), Grand National (April), Monaco Grand Prix (May), Cowes Week (July/August), US Open (September)

4. Westminster Abbey consecrated (1065), Shakespeare born (1564), Gunpowder Plot (1605), Great Fire of London (1666), Battle of Blenheim (1704)

3 points for each in the correct order.

THE WISDOM OF THE CROWD: VICTORIA'S REIGN From page 77.

Queen Victoria reigned for **63** years.

The Ministry takes the middle answer (the median) to represent the Crowd's collective answer, in this case it was 57 ... the Crowd was out by 6 years.

If you guessed between 58 and 68 years, inclusive, you beat the Crowd!

Award yourself points for accuracy as follows:
A guess between 57 and 69, inclusive, 2 points
Or a guess between 60 and 66, inclusive, 5 points
Or a guess between 62 and 65, inclusive, 10 points

SMALL COUNTRIES From page 70.

Answers in order of increasing difficulty:

Vatican City (0.44 km²), Monaco (2.02 km²) (1pt)
San Marino (61 km²), Liechtenstein (160 km²) (2pts)
Maldives (300 km²), Malta (316 km²) (3pts)
Saint Kitts and Nevis (261 km²), Marshall Islands (181 km²) (4pts)
Nauru (21 km²), Tuvalu (26 km²) (5pts)

Add up the points for the answers given, deduct 2 points for any incorrect answer.

CHOICE OF FOUR 9 From page 64.

1. D – A tightrope walker; 2. B – The Underworld; 3. D – Reticulated Python (can grow to 8 metres long); 4. A – Turkey; 5. D – Draco Malfoy (Malfoy disarmed Dumbledore, becoming the wand's owner); 6. B – Peak District (in 1951)

2 points for each correct answer.

PICTURE LOGIC: COUNTRY OUTLINES From page 56.

A. Austria	I. Singapore
B. Kenya	J. Pakistan
C. Cyprus	K. Morocco
D. North Korea	L. Peru
E. Portugal	M. Egypt
F. Finland	N. Germany
G. Laos	O. Croatia
H. Panama	P. Iraq

1. B, K, M	10. C, O
2. E, H, J, L	11. B, L (Kenya
3. A, B, D, H, O	partially, Peru
4. A, C, E, F, N	entirely)
5. A, N	12. J, P
6. C	13. D
7. D, F	14. P
8. A, G	15. A, I, L
9. C, I	16. E, K

2 points for each correct answer.

PUT IN ORDER 2 From page 30.

1. *King Lear* (800 BC), *Julius Caesar* (44–42 BC), *Hamlet* (ninth century), *Macbeth* (1039–1057), *Richard II* (1398–1400).
2. Ann Packer (800m, Tokyo 1964), Steve Redgrave (Coxed Four, Los Angeles 1984), Linford Christie (100m, Barcelona 1992), Christine Ohuruogu (400m, Beijing 2008), Jessica Ennis-Hill (Heptathlon, London 2012).

3. Thames (346km), Shannon (360km), Seine (775km), Rhine (1,230km), Danube (2,850km).
4. United States (1948), France (1972), United Kingdom (1974), Russia (1990), Vietnam (2014).

3 points for each in the correct order.

ODDS AND ENDS 6 From page 39.

1. Donkey Kong; 2. Louis Pasteur; 3. Nakatomi Plaza; 4. *Fried Eggs*; 5. The Aegean; 6. George VI; 7. 21; 8. Harold Wilson (1964–1970 and 1974–1976); 9. Shaking My Head; 10. Montreal 1976 (as Head of State of Canada; The Duke of Edinburgh opened the 1956 Olympics in Melbourne); 11. A Heffalump; 12. 'Screw Steamer' (i.e. driven by a screw propeller); 13. Hartlepool (during the Napoleonic Wars a monkey was hanged in the town as a French spy); 14. Sherlock Holmes; 15. Windsor (*The Merry Wives of Windsor*).

2 points for each correct answer.

MATCHING PAIRS: MOVIE TAGLINES From page 32.

1I, 2J, 3E, 4H, 5C, 6G, 7D, 8K, 9L, 10F, 11B, 12A

1 point for each correct answer. If playing blind, i.e. without looking at the second set, 3 points for each answer.

FOUR CLUES 2 From page 23.

1. 1999
2. Jessica Ennis-Hill
3. *The Talented Mr. Ripley*

Award 5 points for a correct answer from the first clue only, 3 points from the first two clues, 2 points from the first three, 1 point if all four clues were needed.

ODDS AND ENDS 3 From page 17.

1. Palindromes (the word is a palindrome); 2. The sinking of the *Titanic*; 3. Umbrellas; 4. **S**uper **M**assive **B**lack **H**ole; 5. Mongolia; 6. 'Hulk' (the Brazilian footballer, Hulk Hogan, Ruffalo played the Incredible Hulk; 7. 404; 8. Desert Storm; 9. Neapolitan; 10. The size (circumference) of earth; 11. King's Lynn; 12. They have raised marks (home keys); 13. *The Curious Incident of the Dog in the Night-Time*; 14. Strudel; 15. Cabbage.

2 points for each correct answer.

PICTURE LOGIC: SYMBOLS From page 8.

A. Do not tumble-dry
B. Hazardous substance
C. Peace Symbol (Campaign for Nuclear Disarmament)
D. Cancer star sign (the crab)
E. Recycled
F. Drip-dry
G. USB
H. Picnic area (Ordnance Survey symbol)
I. Bluetooth
J. Aries star sign (the ram)
K. Female symbol
L. Extinction Rebellion
M. Toxic
N. Recyclable
O. Do not bleach
P. Beach (Ordnance Survey symbol)

1. B, M
2. A, F, O
3. G, I
4. K
5. C, L
6. D, J
7. H, P
8. A, F
9. I
10. M
11. O
12. E
13. N
14. J, K
15. H
16. P, D

2 points for each correct answer.

1. 'Fairytale of New York' (by The Pogues and Kirsty MacColl)
2. Pakistan
3. 2008

Award 5 points for a correct answer from the first clue only, 3 points from the first two clues, 2 points from the first three, 1 point if all four clues were needed.

1. D – Simon and Garfunkel; 2. C – Panda (42 teeth, a lion has 30, an elephant 26 and a sloth 18); 3. D – Worcester; 4. A – Australia; 5. A – North; 6. B – Melbourne, 1956 (The Queen was unable to travel because of her schedule).

2 points for each correct answer.

1. Bear – the others are types of sharks; 2. Houston is a New York street (running horizontally across the map), the others are avenues (running vertically); 3. Douglas Adams – the others are members of Monty Python; 4. *La Traviata* is by Verdi, the others are by Puccini; 5. The San Francisco Giants are a baseball team, the others are NFL (American Football) teams.

1 point for each correct answer, 2 bonus points for the correct reason.

1. They all can be followed by 'five'; 2. The capital city is the same name as the country; 3. Words containing hidden Greek letters (Beta, Rho, Psi, Iota, Xi); 4. Islands in the Channel Islands archipelago; 5. Accommodation-related words in the titles of Elvis Presley songs ('Baby, Let's Play House', 'Crying in the Chapel', 'Heartbreak Hotel', 'Jailhouse Rock').

3 points for each correct answer.

1. They are/were all (originally) drummers; 2. Snake; 3. Edward the Confessor; 4. E. L. James (the 'Fifty Shades' trilogy); 5. Heat of chillies; 6. The Great Lakes (**H**uron, **O**ntario, **M**ichigan, **E**erie, **S**uperior); 7. Heroin; 8. Tilda Swinton; 9. Sutton Hoo; 10. Lennox Lewis; 11. The Seven Hills of Rome; 12. Chile; 13. Dating trees from rings; 14. Toes; 15. *The Lord of the Rings* (Bilbo Baggins).

2 points for each correct answer.

1. Humidity; 2. Isobar; 3. Wind; 4. Oxygen; 5. A sandstorm; 6. 2 m/s; 7. Cloud cover (one okta corresponds to an eighth of the sky, e.g. 4 oktas indicates the sky is half covered in cloud, at 8 oktas the sky is completely covered in cloud); 8. Exosphere; 9. Katrina; 10. El Niño.

2 points for each correct answer.

2 Across: 1. Kirk Douglas; 2. Group; 3. Flint; 4. Haddock; 5. Bird's eye.

The link is 'CAPTAIN': Captain Kirk, Group Captain, Captain Flint (Long John Silver's parrot), Captain Haddock (a supporting character in *The Adventures of Tintin*), Captain Birdseye.

3 Across: 1. Eyebrow; 2. Lead (*plumbum* in Latin, reflected in its chemical symbol Pb); 3. Case; 4. Skirt; 5. Moustache.

The link is 'PENCIL': Eyebrow pencil, Pencil lead, Pencil case, Pencil skirt, Pencil moustache.

1 Down: 1. California; 2. *Mayflower*; 3. Savoy cabbage; 4. Dorchester; 5. Raffles.

The link is 'HOTEL': 'Hotel California', The Mayflower Hotel (Washington, D.C. hotel, known as the 'Hotel of Presidents'), The Savoy, The Dorchester, Raffles Hotel.

2 Down: 1. Massif; 2. America; 3. Point; 4. Reservation; 5. Glasgow.

The link is 'CENTRAL': Massif Central (highland region in the middle of southern France), Central America, Central point, Central reservation, Glasgow Central (railway station).

1 point for each correct answer. 2 bonus points for each correct link. 5 bonus points for solving the grid.

WHAT COMES NEXT? 7
From page 125.

1. Survive (last words of each line of chorus of 'I Will Survive' by Gloria Gaynor); 2. £120 (Prices of properties on the first street of the Monopoly board . . . Old Kent Road, Whitechapel Road, King's Cross Station, The Angel Islington, Euston Road, Pentonville Road); 3. HBP (Initials of Harry Potter books following 'Harry Potter and the . . .' in order of publication . . . *Philosopher's Stone, Chamber of Secrets, Prisoner of Azkaban, Goblet of Fire, Order of the Phoenix, Half-Blood Prince*); 4. Tiara

(or any five-letter word beginning with 'ti' making a 'tee' sound; five-letter words starting with the syllables assigned to the musical scale – do, re, mi, fa, sol, la, ti); 5. Grew worse (. . . On Friday . . . events in the life of Solomon Grundy according to the nursery rhyme . . . followed by 'Died' and 'Buried' on Saturday/Sunday).

3 points for each correct answer.

ODDS AND ENDS 17 From page 117.

1. Bruce Springsteen; 2. Scorpion; 3. Caithness; 4. Heart; 5. Harry; 6. Shrubbery; 7. Red; 8. Oedipus (they were his parents); 9. India and Sri Lanka; 10. Civilians; 11. Hieroglyphics; 12. 'Knowing Me, Knowing You'; 13. 37; 14. SPQR (Senate and the people of Rome); 15. Grace.

2 points for each correct answer.

PICTURE LOGIC: CHEMICAL ELEMENTS From page 108.

A. Oxygen	I. Lead
B. Mercury	J. Hydrogen
C. Phosphorus	K. Chlorine
D. Zinc	L. Gold
E. Bromine	M. Plutonium
F. Carbon	N. Copper
G. Uranium	O. Nitrogen
H. Argon	P. Sodium

1. A, H, J, K, O	9. A, F, J
2. B, E	10. F
3. G, M	11. K, P
4. D, I, L	12. J
5. B, G, M	13. K
6. B	14. N
7. L	15. C
8. A, H, O	16. H

2 points for each correct answer.

FOUR CLUES 9 From page 153.

1. Clavicle (or collar bone)
2. Ebenezer Scrooge
3. 1995

Award 5 points for a correct answer from the first clue only, 3 points from the first two clues, 2 points from the first three, 1 point if all four clues were needed.

ODDS AND ENDS 15 From page 101.

1. Aberdeen; 2. Midnight; 3. Marcel; 4. Born outside the British Isles (Andrew Bonar Law in New Brunswick, Canada, Boris Johnson in Manhattan, New York City); 5. Echoes (i.e. sound-damped); 6. Twelve (1,4,1,1,4,1); 7. Wakanda; 8. His wife and daughter; 9. They were all killed by their own designs or inventions (Andrews designed the *Titanic*, Heselden was killed in 2010 while riding a Segway, Smolinski was killed in the test flight of his flying car in 1973); 10. Louisiana; 11. Yeti; 12. Iceland; 13. Basmati rice; 14. Alzheimer's disease; 15. Witchcraft (the Witchcraft Act of 1735 was only repealed in 1951).

2 points for each correct answer.

CHOICE OF FOUR 14 From page 94.

1. A – Orthopaedics; 2. C – 65 (19, 21, 25); 3. A – Lionel Messi (2006, 2014, 2018, he turned 31 during the 2018 finals – Pelé just missed the achievement, his 30th birthday came four months after the 1970 finals); 4. A – Crosby Beach; 5. B – Basque Country; 6. C – Montenegro.

2 points for each correct answer.

FOUR CLUES 5 From page 85.

1. 'Get Lucky' (by Daft Punk)
2. 2011
3. Richard III

Award 5 points for a correct answer from the first clue only, 3 points from the first two clues, 2 points from the first three, 1 point if all four clues were needed.

ODDS AND ENDS 11 From page 76.

1. Red Rum (Red Rum won the Grand National for a second consecutive time in 1974, winning in 1973, 1974 and 1977, coming second in 1975 and 1976); 2. Batman; 3. Shuttle; 4. Edinburgh; 5. Sunday; 6. The sight of blood; 7. Peach; 8. Somebody sneezed; 9. Pyramid (built in the desert at Saqqara, near Cairo); 10. Taekwondo; 11. Plantagenet; 12. *Alien*; 13. Polar bear; 14. 1 AD; 15. A fried egg.

2 points for each correct answer.

FORMERLY KNOWN AS . . . From page 70.

1. *Who Wants To Be a Millionaire?*; 2. Victoria Line (**Vic**toria – **King**'s Cross . . . a similar construction to the naming of the Bakerloo line – Baker Street to Waterloo); 3. *Cluedo*; 4. Oslo; 5. *Gone with the Wind*; 6. Times Square; 7. The Sistine Chapel; 8. Newcastle upon Tyne; 9. The United Arab Emirates; 10. *Pride and Prejudice*.

2 points for each correct answer.

CONNECTIONS 7 From page 75.

1. Stroganoff; 2. Ground; 3. The Duke of Wellington; 4. Tomato; 5. Kobe Bryant.

The connection is **beef** – Beef Stroganoff, Ground beef, Beef Wellington, Beef tomato, Kobe beef.

2 points for each correct answer, 5 points for guessing the connection.

1. A – San Marino; 2. B – Mont Sainte-Victoire; 3. A – Tropic of Cancer; 4. B – Chicago (in the song 'My Kind of Town'); 5. C – 80%; 6. D – 1958 (beating Sweden in the final).

2 points for each correct answer.

1. Avocado; 2. Lorna Doone; 3. Ecuador; 4. Prima donna; 5. Radon.

The connection is '**ado**' – the answers all contain the word 'ado'.

2 points for each correct answer, 5 points for guessing the connection.

1. Right (The server and receiver stand on the right side on deuce points; the left side is known as the 'ad court' because the players stand there for advantage points); 2. Windy; 3. Bela Lugosi; 4. Vice Admiral; 5. Edinburgh.

2 points for each correct answer.

1. Hummingbird (*beija flor*); 2. Stormzy; 3. Ada Lovelace; 4. It was made of aluminium; 5. Pantheon; 6. Sphere; 7. Thirteen; 8. YOLO (You only live once); 9. Attorney; 10. Their maiden names are both Bouvier; 11. 10; 12. Devon; 13. Shrew (*The Taming of the Shrew*); 14. Radar; 15. Chanel No. 5.

2 points for each correct answer.

1. Alter egos of Batman villains (The Riddler, The Penguin, Catwoman, Two-Face); 2. Members of cooking/food-related groups (Spice Girls, Red Hot Chili Peppers, The Cranberries, Black Eyed Peas); 3. Words that go with cities to make phrases (Beef Wellington, Berlin Wall, Stockholm Syndrome, Singapore Sling, Tokyo Rose); 4. Words that go with time periods (second fiddle, minute steak, finest hour, May Day, Fashion Week); 5. All connected with 'Olympia' (Olympia is the state capital of Washington and a painting by Manet, Kensington Olympia is a tube station, the 12-metre Statue of Zeus at Olympia was one of the Seven Wonders of the Ancient World).

3 points for each correct answer.

1. St Paul's Cathedral (tallest building in London moving back from the present day); 2. Yoko (last word of the title of The Beatles' last six UK number ones: 'All You Need Is Love', 'Hello Goodbye', 'Lady Madonna', 'Hey Jude', 'Get Back', 'The Ballad of John and Yoko'); 3. Munich (Host cities of Summer Olympic Games from 1950); 4. Tom Thumb, or any phrase with 'thumb' in it (digits – little finger, ring finger, middle finger, index finger, thumb); 5. FOAK (poker hands in increasing order of value: pair, two pair, three of a kind, straight, flush, full house, four of a kind).

3 points for each correct answer.

1. UNICEF; 2. Venice; 3. Viceroy; 4. Magic Eye; 5. Triceratops.

The connection is '**ice**' – the answers all contain the word ice.

2 points for each correct answer, 5 bonus points for guessing the connection.

ODD ONE OUT 11 From page 168.

1. A cherry is a drupe (a fruit with a stone), the others are botanically classed as berries; 2. Commander is a navy rank – the others are army ranks; 3. E sharp is a white note on the piano (it is equivalent to F), the others are black notes; 4. George H. W. Bush served one term as president, the others served two terms; 5. 'After all, tomorrow is another day' is the last line of *Gone with the Wind*, all the others are first lines (*Moby Dick*, *A Christmas Carol*, *1984*, *Rebecca*, respectively).

1 point for each correct answer, 2 bonus points for the correct reason.

LARGE COUNTRIES From page 161.

Answers in order of increasing difficulty:

Russia (17,098,246 km²), Canada (9,984,670 km²) (1pt)
China (9,596,961 km²), United States (9,525,067 km²), Australia (7,692,024 km²), Brazil (8,515,767 km²) (2pts)
India (3,287,263 km²), Kazakhstan (2,724,900 km²) (3pts)
Argentina (2,780,400 km²) (4pts)
Algeria (2,381,741 km²) (5pts)

Add up the points for the answers given, deduct 2 points for any incorrect answer.

LETTER BOX 5 From page 146.

S₁	I	P₂
T₃	O₄	I₅
A₆	C	H

Answer: PISTACHIO

1 point for each correct answer, 5 bonus points for solving the snake.

Notes:

1. Ulysses S. Grant, Harry S. Truman (the middle initial of the former stood for nothing, arising from a clerical error in his congressional appointment).

2. 17th letter of the Greek alphabet, written P or p.

3. Mr T, who played B. A. Baracus in *The A-Team*.

4. The Baltimore Os.

5. *I, Claudius*.

6. Ampere.

WHAT COMES NEXT? 9 From page 139.

1. S (for second . . . Initials of Year, Month, Week, Day, Hour, Minute); 2. Captain James T. Kirk (captains of the *Enterprise*, in chronological order, from *Star Trek*); 3. Nano (decreasing orders of magnitude below one . . . A tenth, hundredth, thousandth, millionth, billionth); 4. California (US states in alphabetical order); 5. Re (red . . . First two letters of snooker colours, decreasing in points value)

3 points for each correct answer.

CONNECTIONS 12 From page 131.

1. *Ex Machina*; 2. Roman; 3. *Much Ado About Nothing*; 4. Scuba; 5. Taxi rank.

The connection is **countries** – the answers contain hidden country names . . . China, Oman, Chad, Cuba, Iran.

2 points for each correct answer, 5 points for guessing the connection.

FIFTY-FIFTY 11 From page 121.

1. Served underarm (Chang was struggling with cramp at the time, the serve surprised and unsettled Lendl and Chang won the

point and later the match); 2. Nudity; 3. Art Nouveau (from 1890 to 1910, Art Deco from around 1910 to 1935); 4. Thirty years (1618–1648); 5. On the left.

2 points for each correct answer.

MATCHING PAIRS: ANAGRAMS OF BRITISH FOOTBALL TEAMS
From page 116.

1D, 2G, 3A, 4L, 5H, 6C, 7J, 8B, 9K, 10F, 11E, 12I

1 point for each correct answer. If playing blind, i.e. without looking at the second set, 3 points for each answer.

CHOICE OF FOUR 16 From page 107.

1. D – Travis Scott; 2. A – Bobby Moore; 3. A – Blessing; 4. B – 8 minutes (8 minutes and 20 seconds); 5. D – Kreacher; 6. B – Gerhard Schröder.

2 points for each correct answer.

PHOBIAS From page 100.

Answers in order of increasing difficulty:

Flying (aerophobia), Spiders (arachnophobia) (1pt)
Heights (acrophobia), Open spaces, confinement, situations in which escape is difficult (agoraphobia) (2pts)
Snakes (ophidiophobia), Injections or needles (trypanophobia) (3pts)
Dogs (cynophobia), Social situations (social phobia) (4pts)
Germs/Dirt (mysophobia), Thunder and lightning (astraphobia) (5pts)

Add up the points for the answers given, deduct 2 points for any incorrect answer.

LINKOPHILIA 3 From page 92.

2 Across: 1. Ray; 2. Blocker; 3. Numeric; 4. Bet; 5. Particles.

The link is 'ALPHA': Alpha ray, Alpha blocker, Alphanumeric, Alphabet, Alpha particles.

3 Across: 1. Arch; 2. Public; 3. 'Blurred Lines'; 4. Within; 5. Mortal.

The link is 'ENEMY': Arch enemy, Public enemy, Enemy lines, Enemy within, Mortal enemy.

1 Down: 1. Family; 2. Valley; 3. Christmas; 4. Medium; 5. Trigger.

The link is 'HAPPY': Happy family, *Happy Valley*, Happy Christmas, Happy medium, Trigger happy.

2 Down: 1. Estate car; 2. Nerve; 3. It's free; 4. Double; 5. Orange.

The link is 'AGENT': Estate agent, Nerve agent, Free agent, Double agent, Agent Orange.

1 point for each correct answer. 2 bonus points for each correct link. 5 bonus points for solving the grid.

DETECTIVES From page 83.

1. Sherlock Holmes (in *His Last Bow* we learn Holmes retired to a farm on the Sussex Downs to become a beekeeper); 2. Thompson Twins; 3. Nordic

noir (or Scandi noir); 4. Columbo;
5. Starsky and Hutch; 6. Idris Elba;
7. Dorset (*Broadchurch*); 8. Miss Marple;
9. *Chinatown*; 10. Helen Mirren.

2 points for each correct answer.

CONNECTIONS 6 From page 63.

1. Beta testing; 2. Gateshead; 3. The Greatest;
4. Roller skates; 5. (Tectonic) Plates.

The connection is '**ates**' – all the answers
contain this group of letters.

2 points for each correct answer, 5 points
for guessing the connection.

CHOICE OF FOUR 10 From page 69.

1. C – Ouse; 2. D – *Twilight* (by Stephenie
Meyer); 3. B – Heart; 4. A – Ed Sheeran
('Photograph'); 5. C – 100,000; 6. D –
Prosecco.

2 points for each correct answer.

MORE, LESS OR THE SAME? 2
From page 63.

1. The fall of the Berlin Wall, which was in
1989 (Mandela was released in 1990).
2. The same – 729.
3. Thomas Hardy wrote 18 recognized
novels (Dickens wrote 15).
4. Chess pieces – each player has 16
(in Backgammon players start with 15
counters).
5. The Shard – has 87 floors (the Chrysler
Building has 77 floors).

3 points for each correct answer.

ODDS AND ENDS 8 From page 54.

1. The Urals; 2. Alibi; 3. Ben Okri; 4. Bill Gates
(they founded Microsoft); 5. Ed Sheeran;
6. General Certificate of Secondary
Education; 7. Two – the Great Pyramid

at Giza and the Lighthouse or Pharos
in Alexandria; 8. Laurel and Hardy; 9. 8
(piccolo = quarter bottle, magnum = two
bottles); 10. 29%; 11. Fen; 12. Venus de Milo;
13. The Forth Bridge; 14. Dita Von Teese;
15. –ing.

2 points for each correct answer.

CHOICE OF FOUR 7 From page 46.

1. C – Take their clothes off (a striptease
artist); 2. C – Bori; 3. A – Delaware; 4. D –
Vatican City (it is no higher than 75 metres
above sea level); 5. C – 'What is your
favourite colour?' (Sir Robin fails at the
'swallow' question); 6. A – Double Decker.

2 points for each correct answer.

POETRY From page 38.

1. 'count the ways'; 2. Six hundred (from
'The Charge of the Light Brigade' by Alfred,
Lord Tennyson); 3. 'Shall I compare thee to
a summer's day?'; 4. Sylvia Plath; 5. A haiku;
6. Runcible; 7. Carol Ann Duffy; 8. W. H.
Auden; 9. 'The Ballad of Reading Gaol' (by
Oscar Wilde); 10. Refrain.

2 points for each correct answer.

RAILWAY STATIONS WITH THREE-LETTER NAMES From page 22.

Answers in order of increasing difficulty:

Ayr (South Ayrshire), Ely (Cambridgeshire)
(1pt)
Par (Cornwall), Rye (East Sussex) (2pts)
Ash (Surrey), Lee (South-east London)
(3pts)
Lye (West Midlands), Ore (East Sussex)
(4pts)
Wye (Kent), Wem (Shropshire) (5pts)

Add up the points for the answers given,
deduct 2 points for any incorrect answer.

HIP HOP AND RAP From page 16.

1. M.I.A.; 2. Jay-Z; 3. N.W.A; 4. Stormzy;
5. Fugees; 6. Kanye West; 7. Drake ('Fancy');
8. 50 Cent; 9. Tinie Tempah; 10. The
Notorious B.I.G.

2 points for each correct answer.

FIFTY-FIFTY 1 From page 7.

1. The Tropic of Cancer (the most northerly
point the sun can be directly overhead);
2. Tomato; 3. Yes; 4. Murder (it is a
parliament of owls); 5. Gary Numan (is 13
days older than Gary Oldman).

2 points for each correct answer.

ODD ONE OUT 12 From page 181.

1. Gypsy is a moth, the others are
butterflies; 2. All are Thames bridges, the
Millennium Bridge is a footbridge, the
others are road bridges; 3. Henry VI was
from the House of Lancaster, the others
were Tudors; 4. Caravaggio was Italian, the
other artists were Dutch; 5. Agoraphobia
is fear of open spaces, the others are fears
of living things (spiders, mice, snakes and
birds, respectively).

1 point for each correct answer, 2 bonus
points for the correct reason.

IN COMMON 12 From page 168.

1. Imperial units (a cable is one-tenth of a
nautical mile, a perch is 16½ feet, equivalent
to a rod, a peck is a dry unit of volume
equivalent to two dry gallons, a drachm is
an eighth of an apothecaries' ounce, a slug
is a unit of mass, defined as the mass that is
accelerated by one foot per second when
a force of one pound is exerted on it);
2. They are all capes; 3. Ministries in George
Orwell's *1984*; 4. Movies that are questions

(*What Ever Happened to Baby Jane?*, *Guess
Who's Coming to Dinner*, *Dude, Where's
My Car?*, *Who Framed Roger Rabbit*);
5. Types of jackets.

3 points for each correct answer.

ODDS AND ENDS 24 From page 160.

1. Anthony Daniels; 2. Cake; 3. Montana;
4. Fire; 5. *North by Northwest*; 6. David
Lloyd George (he spoke Welsh); 7. Margaret
Atwood; 8. Chess; 9. Elephant dung;
10. Plum; 11. Napoleon; 12. Sherwood Forest;
13. Zinc; 14. Elton John; 15. Lowestoft.

2 points for each correct answer.

US PRESIDENTS CALLED JAMES OR JOHN From page 152.

Answers in order of increasing difficulty:

John F. Kennedy (1pt)
John Adams, James Madison (2pts)
James Monroe, John Quincy Adams, Jimmy
Carter (3pts)
James A. Garfield, James K. Polk, James
Buchanan (4pts)
John Tyler (5pts)

Add up the points for the answers given,
deduct 2 points for any incorrect answer.

MATCHING PAIRS: FANDOMS From page 145.

1J, 2F, 3K, 4G, 5I, 6L, 7D, 8B, 9A, 10C, 11E, 12H

1 point for each correct answer. If playing
blind, i.e. without looking at the second set,
3 points for each answer.

THE WISDOM OF THE CROWD: HADRIAN'S WALL From page 138.

Hadrian's Wall is **73** miles long.

The Ministry takes the middle answer
(the median) to represent the Crowd's

collective answer, in this case it was 73 . . . the Crowd was correct! The 30 and under cohort also were correct.

If you guessed 73, you matched the Crowd!

Award points for accuracy as follows:
A guess between 66 and 80, inclusive, 2 points
Or a guess between 69 and 77, inclusive, 5 points
Or a guess of between 71 and 75, inclusive, 10 points

FIFTY-FIFTY 12 From page 131.

1. K-Pop (i.e. Korean); 2. Two 1p coins (7.12g, a 10p coin weighs 6.5g); 3. A netball court (30.5m by 15.25m, a basketball court is 28.7m by 15.2m); 4. Insects; 5. *Puss in Boots*.

2 points for each correct answer.

PUT IN ORDER 9 From page 148.

1. Stapes (3mm), Metatarsal (50mm), Clavicle (150mm), Ulna (270mm), Femur (500mm)
2. St David's Day (1 March), St Patrick's Day (17 March), May Day (first Monday in May), Labor Day (first Monday in September), Thanksgiving (final Thursday in November)
3. Tinie Tempah (6 number ones as of 2021), Spice Girls (9), Take That (12), Madonna (13), The Beatles (17)
4. Mark Spitz (1972), Nadia Comăneci (1976), Michael Johnson (1996), Cathy Freeman (2004), Usain Bolt (2008)

3 points for each in the correct order.

AFRICA From page 123.

1. Khartoum; 2. Sierra Leone; 3. Egypt (7 times, at time of publishing); 4. Liberia (Monrovia); 5. They are extreme points of the African mainland – north, east, south

and west; 6. Jenga; 7. Nelson Mandela; 8. The Zambezi; 9. Mogadishu; 10. 12.30.

2 points for each correct answer.

INSECTS From page 118.

1. Moths; 2. Nymph; 3. Thorax; 4. Waggle dance; 5. Eats them; 6. Beetle; 7. Cockroach; 8. Bees; 9. Praying mantis (the European mantis, or *Mantis religiosa*, is so named because its front legs are held in a distinctive posture, as if in prayer); 10. Adam Ant.

2 points for each correct answer.

LETTER BOX 4 From page 106.

L_1	E	Y
I	I	L_2
D	N_3	A

Answer: LEYLANDII (or the Leyland cypress, a fast-growing hybrid tree created by Christopher Leyland)

1 point for each correct answer, 5 bonus points for solving the snake.

Notes:
1. L. Ron Hubbard, founder of the Church of Scientology.
2. L-plate, for a learner driver.
3. Newton.

ODD ONE OUT 7 From page 100.

1. The Radius is a bone in the arm, the others are found in the leg; 2. Vanuatu is in the Pacific, the others are countries in Africa; 3. Rothko's *Orange and Red on Red* is predominantly red, all the other paintings are predominantly blue; 4. Elinor Dashwood is from Jane Austen (*Sense and Sensibility*), the others are characters from Dickens; 5. Chesley Sullenberger is a pilot

who crash-landed a plane on the Hudson River; the others fear or prefer not to fly.

1 point for each correct answer, 2 bonus points for the correct reason.

FIFTY-FIFTY 8 From page 83.

1. Clockwise (other climbers, like bindweed or runner beans, climb anti-clockwise); 2. Panther; 3. Spider-Man; 4. Stage left (i.e. to the right as seen from the audience); 5. Saint Helena (Napoleon escaped from Elba to fight at Waterloo).

2 points for each correct answer.

MATCHING PAIRS: NAUTICAL ORIGINATING PHRASES From page 74.

1K ('Let the cat out of the bag', referring to the cat-o'-nine-tails.)
2E ('Pipe down', after the practice of the bosun sounding the whistle to indicate lights out.)
3H ('Over a barrel', after the practice of flogging a victim tied to a barrel.)
4A ('Foot loose and fancy free'; the bottom of the mainsail is called the foot, if it is loose it flaps around and is difficult to control.)
5G ('The cut of one's jib', after the cut, meaning condition, of the jib, a sail.)
6B ('Hard and fast', beached firmly on land.)
7I ('Loose cannon', a rogue or disruptive person, if a cannon becoming loose on a gun deck creates chaos for the ship.)
8J ('Show one's true colours'; sometimes a ship may deceive by flying false colours, i.e. its flag.)
9C ('By and large', good in any situation; 'by' means going against the wind, 'large' with the wind.)
10L ('Batten down the hatches', prepare for a storm.)

11D ('Touch and go'; if a ship touches the bottom, and then goes, it's a precarious situation.)
12F ('Hand over fist', the action of hauling a rope.)

1 point for each correct answer. If playing blind, i.e. without looking at the second set, 3 points for each answer.

IN COMMON 5 From page 68.

1. Venues that have hosted the FA Cup Final (The Oval hosted the first cup final in 1872; it was held at various locations including Crystal Palace and Bramall Lane, in Sheffield in 1912, until moving to a permanent home Wembley Stadium in 1923. The Principality Stadium, then called the Millennium Stadium, hosted it between 2001 and 2006 when the new Wembley Stadium was being built); 2. Currencies (Ecuador, Mongolia, Costa Rica, Albania, South/North Korea); 3. People appearing on the Bank of England £10 note; 4. Countries prefixed by 'the'; 5. Words in titles of pantomimes (*Snow White*, *Puss in Boots*, *Ali Baba and the Forty Thieves*, *Mother Goose*, *Babes in the Wood*).

3 points for each correct answer.

MAGIC SQUARE 2 From page 62.

20$_a$	6$_b$	7	17$_c$
9	15$_d$	14	12
13$_e$	11	10	16
8$_f$	18	19	5$_g$

The Magic Number is 50, from the clue take your pick of *Hawaii 5-0*, or the 50th state of the Union.

1 point for each correct answer, 5 bonus points for finding the Magic Number.

Notes:

a. A Nebuchadnezzar is 15 litres, or 20 x 750ml bottles.

b. Italy has borders with Austria, France, San Marino, Slovenia, Switzerland, Vatican City.

c. A haiku is structured 5-7-5.

d. 'Fifteen men on a dead man's chest, yo-ho-ho and a bottle of rum!' from *Treasure Island*.

e. Baker's dozen, i.e. 13.

f. A furlong is 220 yards.

g. Mary Tudor reigned from 1553 until 1558.

THE WISDOM OF THE CROWD: PROPERTIES IN MONOPOLY
From page 53.

There are **28** properties in the game of Monopoly.

(There are 22 that can be developed with houses and hotels, 2 utilities and 4 stations.)

The Ministry takes the middle answer (the median) to represent the Crowd's collective answer, in this case it was 28 . . . the Crowd was correct!

If you guessed 28, you matched the Crowd!

Award points for accuracy as follows:
A guess between 25 and 31, inclusive, 2 points
Or a guess between 27 and 29, inclusive, 5 points
Or a guess of exactly 28, 10 points

COCKTAILS From page 33.

1. Singapore Sling; 2. Pina Colada; 3. 'Gin and Juice'; 4. Cranberry juice; 5. Pornstar Martini; 6. Mai Tai; 7. Tequila; 8. Gin; 9. Bellini; 10. Brazil.

2 points for each correct answer.

PLACES IN SONG LYRICS 1
From page 36.

1L ('Vienna', Ultravox)
2K ('Streets of Philadelphia', Bruce Springsteen)
3H ('Galway Girl', Ed Sheeran)
4F San Francisco ('Be Sure to Wear Flowers in Your Hair', Scott McKenzie)
5A ('One Night in Bangkok', Murray Head)
6J ('No Sleep till Brooklyn', The Beastie Boys)
7D Memphis ('Honky Tonk Women', The Rolling Stones)
8E Brighton ('Pinball Wizard', The Who)
9B Miami ('Back in the USSR', The Beatles)
10G Birmingham ('Panic', The Smiths)
11I ('Havana', Camila Cabello)
12C Liverpool ('Rotterdam', The Beautiful South)

2 points for each correct answer, 1 bonus point each for knowing the song/artist.

CONNECTIONS 2 From page 19.

1. Apple; 2. Bread; 3. Worcestershire; 4. HP; 5. Mint.

The connection is **sauce** – apple sauce, bread sauce, Worcestershire sauce, HP sauce, mint sauce.

2 points for each correct answer, 5 points for guessing the connection.

ODD ONE OUT 2 From page 22.

1. *Mansfield Park* is by Jane Austen, the others are by the Brontë sisters; 2. Linguini is a flattened strip of pasta, the others are stuffed pastas; 3. Monica (in *Friends*) is Ross's sister, the others have been married to him; 4. Dushanbe is the capital of Tajikistan in Asia, the others are capitals of African countries (Democratic Republic of the Congo, Tanzania, Nigeria); 5. A rolling

hitch fixes a rope to something, the other knots join two ropes together.

1 point for each correct answer, 2 bonus points for the correct reason.

PUT IN ORDER 1 From page 15.

1. Lancaster, Grimsby, Leicester, St Albans, Swindon.
2. 'Is this the real life?', 'Mama, just killed a man', 'Galileo Figaro', 'Beelzebub has a devil put aside for me', 'Can't do this to me, baby'.
3. Salt (NaCl), Water (H_2O), Sulphuric acid (H_2SO_4), Ethanol (C_2H_6O), Caffeine ($C_8H_{10}N_4O_2$).
4. (Three) French hens, (Seven) Swans a-swimming, (Eight) Maids a-milking, (Nine) Ladies dancing, (Eleven) Pipers piping.

3 points for each in the correct order.

CHOICE OF FOUR 1 From page 6.

1. C – Fox; 2. A – Greece; 3. B – Postcode; 4. B – Tennessee; 5. C – Third; 6. D – Tomatoes.

2 points for each correct answer.

PUT IN ORDER 6 From page 91.

1. Snooker (52.5mm diameter), Tennis (65–68mm), Hockey (71–74mm), Polo (76–89mm), Softball (97.1mm).
2. Signing of the Magna Carta (1215), Habeas Corpus Act (1679), Abolition of slavery in the US (1865), Universal declaration of human rights (1948), 'I have a dream' speech (Martin Luther King, Jr, 1963).
3. *Who Framed Roger Rabbit* ($58 million); *Titanic* ($200m), *Spectre* ($230m), *Harry Potter and the Half-Blood Prince* ($250m), *Avengers: Endgame* ($356m).

4. Dwarf Willow (0.06m), Olive (10m), Oak (35m), Douglas Fir (76m), Coast Redwood (112m).

3 points for each in the correct order.

ODDS AND ENDS 25 From page 167.

1. Sixty-six; 2. Battle of Sedgemoor; 3. Turkey; 4. Four; 5. RMS *Titanic*; 6. Squirrel; 7. Carbohydrate; 8. Mount McKinley; 9. Genus; 10. Barcelona; 11. Cadfael; 12. Bonnie Prince Charlie; 13. Clouds; 14. Kenya; 15. Minerva.

2 points for each correct answer.

WHAT COMES NEXT? 11
From page 152.

1. Prince Philip, Duke of Edinburgh (royal consorts, coming forward towards the present day); 2. Femur (largest five bones in the human body in order of size); 3. Lady Gaga/Bradley Cooper (lead actors in versions of *A Star is Born* – 1937, 1954, 1976, 2018); 4. Fifth (New York avenues running east to west); 5. 'Rag bag men' . . . Or any anagram of 'Beggar Man' (anagrams of Tinker, Tailor, Soldier, Sailor, Rich Man, Poor Man).

3 points for each correct answer.

DISNEY AND PIXAR From page 144.

1. Buzz Lightyear; 2. *102 Dalmatians*; 3. Sadness; 4. *Snow White and the Seven Dwarfs*; 5. They are superheroes (*The Incredibles*); 6. Dory; 7. *Frozen*; 8. Thumper; 9. *Pocahontas*; 10. *WALL-E*.

2 points for each correct answer.

CHOICE OF FOUR 20 From page 137.

1. D – Tennis balls; 2. A – Blue; 3. A – Fish; 4. C – The Fall of the Berlin Wall; 5. B – A

flowering plant (*Lysimachia nummularia* or 'creeping Jenny'); 6. B – Great Britain.

2 points for each correct answer.

ODDS AND ENDS 19 From page 130.

1. One; 2. Hannah Montana; 3. Flags; 4. Peninsula; 5. Auckland (1,347 miles from Sydney); 6. 'En croute'; 7. Bring Up the Bodies (they were regarded as already dead); 8. Overwork or exhaustion; 9. Sloe; 10. Sri Lanka; 11. Trebuchet; 12. Frank Sinatra; 13. It was shared between all the nominees (Lawrence Abu Hamdan, Helen Cammock, Oscar Murillo and Tai Shani); 14. SOS (the international distress signal); 15. If someone is a Replicant (from *Blade Runner*).

2 points for each correct answer.

CONNECTIONS 14 From page 156.

1. Jerusalem artichoke; 2. The Hundred Years' War; 3. Panama hat; 4. New bridge; 5. Chinese Checkers.

The connection is **misnomers** – Jerusalem artichoke has no connection with Jerusalem and is not an artichoke, the Hundred Years' War lasted 116 years, Panama hats actually come from Ecuador, Pont Neuf is the oldest bridge on the Seine, Chinese Checkers is not a form of checkers, and it originated in Germany, not China.

2 points for each correct answer, 5 points for guessing the connection.

CLUEDOKU 4 From page 115.

9	1ₐ	8
5_b	3	4
2_c	7	6_d

Notes:
a. South Korea only borders North Korea.
b. (Just slip out the back) Jack, (Make a new plan) Stan, (You don't need to be coy) Roy, (Hop on the bus) Gus, (Just drop off the key) Lee.
c. Two violins, one viola, one cello.
d. Russia, Canada, China, USA, Brazil, Australia.

2 points for each correct answer.

CONNECTIONS 9 From page 99.

1. Vertigo; 2. Chicago; 3. Beethoven; 4. Metropolis; 5. Parasite.

The connection is **one-word movies**.

2 points for each correct answer, 5 points for guessing the connection.

MORE, LESS OR THE SAME? 3 From page 103.

1. A football team has 11 players (a baseball team has 9).
2. The same – 4 in each period (Clement Attlee, Winston Churchill, Anthony Eden, Harold Macmillan in the 1950s, Gordon Brown, David Cameron, Theresa May, Boris Johnson in the 2010s).
3. Countries in Africa – there are 54 (there are 48 countries in Asia).
4. Pluto has 5 moons (Charon, Nix, Hydra, Kerberos and Styx; Mars has 2 – Phobos and Deimos).
5. The same – 5 in each foot/hand.

3 points for each correct answer.

ODDS AND ENDS 12 From page 82.

1. Replicants; 2. Michelle Obama; 3. Bones; 4. The Grand National; 5. 'The boy stood on the burning deck'; 6. They all died while working (Tommy Cooper and Eric Morecambe suffered heart attacks on

stage, Steve Irwin was stung by a stingray while filming); 7. Shakespeare; 8. Mice; 9. *To Kill a Mockingbird* (Harper Lee); 10. Father and son (John Adams/John Quincy Adams and George H. W. Bush/George W. Bush); 11. *Little Red Riding Hood*; 12. Copyright; 13. The Angel of the North; 14. Ferrari (F1 Team); 15. Constantinople.

2 points for each correct answer.

FIFTY-FIFTY 7 From page 78.

1. Sydneysider; 2. Mr Darcy (described having an income of 10,000 pounds a year, double Mr Bingley's income of 5,000 pounds); 3. The Forth Bridge (opened 1890, Tower Bridge opened in 1894); 4. Turkey; 5. The Pink Panther.

2 points for each correct answer.

IN COMMON 6 From page 89.

1. Countries minus first letter (Greece, Spain, Oman, Finland, Iran); 2. Take That (first names of band members disguised in footballers' names); 3. Playing Cards (names of playing cards combine with these words to make phrases . . . Top ten, Every man jack, Drag queen, King prawn, Ace Ventura); 4. Beatrix Potter (Names in Beatrix Potter books . . . Peter Rabbit, Benjamin Bunny, Jeremy Fisher, Tom Kitten, Jemima Puddle-Duck); 5. Cities that span two continents.

3 points for each correct answer.

WHAT COMES NEXT? 4 From page 68.

1. Giving (last words from each line of the rhyme 'Monday's child . . . Friday's child is loving and giving'); 2. Bolt (Usain Bolt . . . winners of men's 100m at the Olympics from 1992); 3. Uxbridge (Constituencies of consecutive British Prime Ministers . . .

Tony Blair, Gordon Brown, David Cameron, Theresa May, Boris Johnson); 4. NTTD (Initials of Daniel Craig Bond films in order of release . . . *Casino Royale, Quantum of Solace, Skyfall, Spectre, No Time to Die*); 5. Lydia (Bennet sisters from *Pride and Prejudice* in reverse order of age).

3 points for each correct answer.

ELEMENTS WITH SYMBOLS DIFFERENT FROM THEIR NAMES From page 61.

Answers in order of increasing difficulty:

Sodium (Na), Gold (Au) (1pt)
Lead (Pb), Iron (Fe) (2pts)
Silver (Ag), Potassium (K) (3pts)
Mercury (Hg), Tin (Sn) (4pts)
Antimony (Sb), Tungsten (W) (5pts)

Add up the points for the answers given, deduct 2 points for any incorrect answer.

CONNECTIONS 5 From page 52.

1. Bumblebee; 2. Fancy; 3. Navigator; 4. Phoenix; 5. Spanish Steps.

The connection is **flights** – 'Flight of the Bumblebee', flight of fancy, *Flight of the Navigator* (1986 film), *Flight of the Phoenix* (2004 film), a flight of steps.

2 points for each correct answer, 5 points for guessing the connection.

MATCHING PAIRS: US PRESIDENTS AND EVENTS IN HISTORY From page 44.

1I (1803), 2E (1968), 3A (1986), 4F (1941), 5B (1962), 6C (1863), 7H (1920), 8J (2008), 9K (1969–72), 10L (1876), 11D (1975), 12G (2020)

1 point for each correct answer. If playing blind, i.e. without looking at the second set, 3 points for each answer.

1. Gallery – others are web browsers;
2. Harlem – is a neighbourhood of Manhattan, others are boroughs of New York City; 3. French horn is in the brass section, others are woodwind; 4. Borneo – all are islands, but Borneo is part of Indonesia, others are sovereign nations in their own right; 5. Ginger – all the others can be used to make milk.

1 point for each correct answer, 2 bonus points for the correct reason.

There are **26** vertebrae in the human spine.

There are 24 pre-sacral vertebrae, separated by intervertebral discs (7 cervical, 12 thoracic and 5 lumbar), plus the bones of the sacrum and coccyx (tailbone). The sacrum and coccyx originally contain 5 and 4 vertebrae respectively, but these are usually fused into single bones in adults.

The Ministry takes the middle answer (the median) to represent the Crowd's collective answer, in this case 26 . . . the Crowd was correct!

If you guessed 26, you matched the Crowd!

Award points for accuracy as follows:
A guess between 23 and 29, inclusive, 2 points
Or a guess between 25 and 27, inclusive, 5 points
Or a guess of exactly 26, 10 points

1. Malibu; 2. Santiago; 3. The Sharks; 4. Beckham (9 to Rooney's 7); 5. Crab.

2 points for each correct answer.

16	2_a	3_b	13_c
5_d	11	10_e	8_f
9_g	7_h	6	12_i
4_j	14	15	1_k

The Magic Number is 34, found in *Miracle on 34th Street*.

1 point for each correct answer, 5 bonus points for finding the Magic Number.

Notes:
a. *The Two Gentlemen of Verona*, by Shakespeare.
b. Tighthead prop wears shirt number 3.
c. Tent hire = thirteen.
d. Henry VII, Henry VIII, Edward VI, Mary I, Elizabeth II (Lady Jane Grey is disputed).
e. Mohs scale goes from talc (1) to diamond (10).
f. Austria has borders with the Czech Republic, Slovakia, Hungary, Slovenia, Italy, Switzerland, Liechtenstein, Germany.
g. As Hercules found, the number can be variable, a Hydra regenerates two heads for each that is chopped off, but is generally taken to be nine.
h. Baker Street, Bank, Barbican, Bayswater, Blackfriars, Bond Street, Borough.
i. *Twelve Angry Men*, 1957 film starring Henry Fonda.
j. A composite number is a natural number created by multiplying two prime numbers together, the smallest prime is number is 2, so the smallest composite number is 4.
k. 'Bring Your Daughter to the Slaughter' is Iron Maiden's only UK number one.

1. Mormons – the others are nicknames of football teams (Darlington FC, Bury FC, Plymouth Argyle FC); 2. Bodmin Moor – the others are National Parks; 3. Sister – the others are in the titles of *Carry On* films; 4. Garlic – is a bulb, the others are roots; 5. Malta – is a true island, the others are part of the mainland.

1 point for each correct answer, 2 bonus points for the correct reason.

1. New Orleans
2. Kamala Harris
3. 2016

Award 5 points for a correct answer from the first clue only, 3 points from the first two clues, 2 points from the first three, 1 point if all four clues were needed.

1. 'Don't Look Back in Anger', Oasis ('And so, Sally can wait/She knows it's too late as we're walking on by'); 2. 'Teenage Dirtbag', Wheatus ('Yeah, I'm just a teenage dirtbag baby/Listen to Iron Maiden baby with me'); 3. 'Like a Virgin', Madonna ('Like a virgin, touched for the very first time'); 4. 'Roar', Katy Perry ('I got the eye of the tiger/A fighter/ Dancing through the fire'); 5. 'Rocket Man', Elton John ('And I think it's gonna be a long long time').

3 points for each correct answer.

1. Women; 2. Saffron; 3. Bird (a seabird, closely related to the gannet); 4. 'Talk less, smile more'; 5. Peking Man.

2 points for each correct answer.

2 Across: 1. Boom; 2. Mr Jelly; 3. Bush (George H. W. and George W.); 4. Monitor lizard; 5. Meteor shower.

The link is 'BABY': Baby boom, Jelly baby, Bushbaby, Baby monitor, Baby shower.

4 Across: 1. Split infinitive; 2. Republic; 3. Skin; 4. Bread (Lavash is an Armenian flatbread, Rugbrød is Danish rye bread, Pistolet is a Belgian bread roll); 5. Belt.

The link is 'BANANA': Banana split, Banana republic, Banana skin, Banana bread, Banana belt (a banana belt is an area within a larger area that enjoys warmer conditions, for instance a microclimate).

1 Down: 1. Book (International Standard Book Number); 2. University; 3. The Vatican; 4. Mobile; 5. Cards (red and yellow).

The link is 'LIBRARY': Library book, University library, Vatican Library, mobile library, Library card.

3 Down: 1. Jumping (jumping spider); 2. Mr; 3. Pinto (the petrol tank of the Ford Pinto was located between the rear axle and rear bumper, creating a fire risk in a rear-end collision. Ford were aware of the problem, but in a controversial memo that became public, calculated the cost of potential litigation was less than the cost of redesigning the car and so did not correct the fault); 4. The (Norfolk) Broads; 5. The kidney.

The link is 'BEAN': Jumping bean, *Mr Bean*, Pinto bean, Broad bean, Kidney bean.

1 point for each correct answer. 2 bonus points for each correct link. 5 bonus points for solving the grid.

THE WISDOM OF THE CROWD: YEARS TO REACH THE MOON
From page 151.

There were **66** years between the Wright Brothers' first powered flight (1903) and Neil Armstrong setting foot on the Moon (1969).

The Ministry takes the middle answer (the median) to represent the Crowd's collective answer, in this case it was 48 . . . the Crowd was out by 18 years.

If you guessed between 49 and 83, inclusive, you beat the Crowd!

Award points for accuracy as follows:
A guess between 59 and 73, inclusive, 2 points
Or a guess between 69 and 77, inclusive, 5 points
Or a guess between 65 and 67, inclusive, 10 points

WHAT COMES NEXT? 10
From page 144.

1. D/32 (Types of musical notes . . . Semibreve is a whole note, minim a half note. Crotchet a quarter, quaver an eighth, semiquaver a sixteenth, demisemiquaver a one thirty-second note); 2. Louisa (Von Trapp children in increasing order of age); 3. Vauxhall (Thames bridges moving inland); 4. Andropov (Leaders of the Soviet Union); 5. 'Generic Pigs' (or any anagram of 'Ginger Spice' . . . these are anagrams of the Spice Girls . . . Posh Spice, Scary Spice, Baby Spice, Sporty Spice).

3 points for each correct answer.

IN COMMON 9 From page 136.

1. Elements named after them (Einsteinium, Mendelevium, Curium, Thorium, Neptunium); 2. They are all Alps; 3. Repeated letter initials (A.A. Milne, B.B. King, SS Great Britain, ZZ Top); 4. People who have given their names to cocktails (Mary Pickford is a prohibition-era cocktail named after the Canadian–American film actress. A Rob Roy is similar to a Manhattan but made with Scotch whisky. Mary Tudor was nicknamed Bloody Mary); 5. Names in titles of *Carry On* films.

3 points for each correct answer.

PUT IN ORDER 10 From page 174.

1. Rome (1960), Mexico City (1968), Seoul (1988), Barcelona (1992), Beijing (2008)
2. Roadrunner (20mph), Rabbit (30mph), Ostrich (45mph), Swordfish (60mph), Cheetah (70mph)
3. Building of the Great Pyramid at Giza (c. 3000 BC), First Olympiad in Greece (776 BC), Alexander defeats Darius III (331 BC at the Battle of Gaugamela), Death of Julius Caesar (44 BC), Birth of Mohammad (570 AD)
4. Shepherd's Bush, Notting Hill Gate, Oxford Circus, Bank, Stratford

3 points for each in the correct order.

PLACES IN SONG LYRICS 2
From page 128.

1 I ('Fairytale of New York', The Pogues and Kirsty MacColl)
2 J Bombay/Mumbai ('Come Fly with Me', Frank Sinatra)
3 A ('Viva Las Vegas', Elvis Presley)
4 C ('Scarborough Fair / Canticle', Simon and Garfunkel)
5 L Atlanta ('Love Shack', The B-52s)
6 G Munich ('Pop Muzik', M)

7H London ('Sultans of Swing', Dire Straits)
8K LA ('All I Wanna Do', Sheryl Crow)
9B ('Rome Wasn't Built in a Day', Morcheeba)
10F Chicago ('Smooth Operator', Sade)
11D Glasgow ('Super Trouper', ABBA)
12E ('Istanbul (Not Constantinople)', They Might Be Giants)

2 points for each correct answer, 1 bonus point each for knowing the artist/song.

ODDS AND ENDS 18 From page 122.

1. Crookshanks; 2. The triathlon; 3. Lionel Richie; 4. Battenberg; 5. The first spacewalk; 6. IKEA; 7. Birmingham (B); 8. His billy; 9. 'I Got You Babe' (Sonny & Cher); 10. 'Nessun dorma'; 11. Guinness; 12. Lucian Freud; 13. At 406m above sea level it is the highest elevation navigable that a boat can reach from the sea; 14. John is first followed by Ringo, Paul and George; 15. Carrot.

2 points for each correct answer.

CHOICE OF FOUR 17 From page 114.

1. C – Mongolia; 2. B – *East of Eden* ('the winter of our discontent' is Shakespeare, 'mice and men' is Burns. Another of Steinbeck's novels, *The Grapes of Wrath*, is also a biblical reference); 3. A – European architecture; 4. B – Manchester; 5. D – Vein; 6. C – Raspberry.

2 points for each correct answer.

WHAT COMES NEXT? 6 From page 106.

1. Deuteronomy (books in the Old Testament); 2. Stumped (cricketing dismissals in decreasing order of frequency); 3. X (Roman numerals in alphabetical order); 4. The World Trade Center (the world's tallest building, going backwards from 2021); 4. Re (Reagan . . . US Presidents' first two letters of surname, going backwards from 2021)

3 points for each correct answer.

PUT IN ORDER 4 From page 71.

1. Pelé FIFA World Cup wins (3), Sebastian Vettel Formula 1 championships (4), Tom Brady Super Bowl wins (7), Jack Nicklaus golf Majors (18), Serena Williams Grand Slam singles titles (23), all as of 2021
2. *His Dark Materials* (Philip Pullman, 3 books), *Twilight* (Stephenie Meyer, 4 books), *Percy Jackson and the Olympians* (Rick Riordan, 5 books), *The Chronicles of Narnia* (C. S. Lewis, 7 books), *Discworld* (Terry Pratchett, 41 books)
3. 'Friday night and the lights are low', 'Night is young and the music's high', 'And when you get the chance', 'Young and sweet, only seventeen', 'Feel the beat from the tambourine'
4. Joseph Stalin (1924–53), Nikita Khrushchev (1953–64), Leonid Brezhnev (1964–82), Yuri Andropov (1982–84), Mikhail Gorbachev (1985–91)

3 points for each in the correct order.

JANE AUSTEN From page 99.

1. *Sense and Sensibility* (1811); 2. Emma Woodhouse; 3. Mr Wickham; 4. *Sanditon*; 5. Charles Darwin; 6. Anne Hathaway; 7. Alison Steadman; 8. *Sense and Sensibility*; 9. *Mansfield Park*; 10. Mr Darcy (Darcin).

2 points for each correct answer.

CHOICE OF FOUR 13 From page 90.

1. B – Germs; 2. A – Burrito; 3. B – Salt (Sodium Chloride); 4. A – Leonardo da Vinci; 5. A – Hastings; 6. D – Uganda

2 points for each correct answer.

1. Tetrahedron (4), Triangular Prism (5), Cube (6), Octahedron (8), Dodecahedron (12)
2. Rydal Water (0.3km²), Buttermere (0.9km²), Coniston Water (4km²), Ullswater (8.9km²), Windermere (14.7km²)
3. Sandro Botticelli (1445–1510), Rembrandt (1606–1669), Thomas Gainsborough (1727–1788), Vincent van Gogh (1853–1890), Mark Rothko (1903–1970)
4. Destiny's Child (3 members), The Killers (4), Arcade Fire (6), Madness (7), Kool and the Gang (14)

3 points for each in the correct order.

A. Richard II
B. Henry VIII
C. Elizabeth II
D. George III
E. George VI
F. Henry V
G. Victoria
H. Mary II
I. Edward IV
J. Anne
K. Elizabeth I
L. John
M Richard III
N. Richard I
O. William III
P. Henry VI

1. A, F, I, L, M, N, P
2. B, F, P
3. H & O ('William and Mary')
4. F, P
5. D, E
6. A, M, N
7. 15 (2+8+2+3)
8. C (Elizabeth II visited China in 1986)
9. H & J, L & N (Mary and Anne were daughters of James II, Richard and John were sons of Henry II)
10. I, P (Henry regained the throne from Edward in 1470, losing it 6 months later after the Battle of Tewkesbury ended the Wars of the Roses with the defeat of the Lancastrians and Henry himself dead in the Tower)
11. C, D, G (Elizabeth II since 1952, George III 59 years, Victoria 63 years)
12. D, P
13. G, J, L (Victoria, Anne, John)
14. D, G
15. L (in 1215)
16. D, M, O

2 points for each correct answer.

1. A – Ear; 2. B – Power station; 3. B – Fifth Avenue; 4. C – Madonna; 5. A – Minotaur; 6. D – 1,000,000.

2 points for each correct answer.

Answers in order of increasing difficulty:

West Germany/Germany, Brazil, Netherlands, France (1pt)
Italy, Argentina (2pts)
Croatia, Hungary (3pts)
Sweden (4pts)
Czechoslovakia (5pts)

Add up the points for the answers given, deduct 2 points for any incorrect answer.

1. Afghanistan and China (3.5 hours); 2. UTC; 3. 7 (also accept one . . . the train and all the stations on the route remain on Moscow time); 4. October (it has 31 days but with the time change from BST to GMT is an hour longer than January, May, July, August and December and two hours longer than March); 5. 12 a.m. – the ISS is on Greenwich Mean Time; 6. China; 7. Iceland, Ireland and Portugal (although Iceland does not observe daylight saving time); 8. Eastern Standard Time (the time zone of the Eastern states of the US); 9. Daylight saving time; 10. 6 a.m. (Argentina 3 hours behind GMT, Ethiopia 3 hours ahead).

2 points for each correct answer.

1. Elizabeth Hurley; 2. Disneyland Paris (gets around 10 million visitors a year, the Eiffel Tower gets around 7 million); 3. Loose Head Prop (Tight Head takes number 3); 4. Munro (Munros are Scottish peaks higher than 3,000 feet, named after a list compiled by Sir Hugh Munro in 1891. Corbetts are Scottish peaks between 2,500 and 3,000 feet, this time after a list compiled by John Rooke Corbett in the 1920s); 5. Red (the red pill is reality, blue is ignorance).

2 points for each correct answer.

Answers in order of increasing difficulty:

Bowled, Caught, Leg Before Wicket (1pt)
Run Out, Stumped (2pts)
Hit Wicket (3pts)
Handled the Ball, Hit the Ball Twice (4pts)
Obstructing the Field, Timed Out (5pts)

Add up the points for the answers given, deduct 2 points for any incorrect answer.

1. All have given names hidden in them – Philip, Olivia, Gary, Ken, Tina; 2. UK number ones with Justin Bieber ('Cold Water', 'Despacito', 'I Don't Care', 'I'm the One'); 3. Largest satellite of each of the planets (Earth, Mars, Jupiter, Saturn, Uranus, Neptune); 4. English/British monarchs with no regnal number, since they are the first and only monarch with that name; 5. All are ingredients in the witches' cauldron in *Macbeth*.

3 points for each correct answer.

1. D – Cara Delevingne (she is god-daughter to Joan Collins); 2. D – Henry IV (first of the line of the House of Lancaster); 3. B – A coming-of-age story; 4. C – Bellingshausen Sea (in the Southern Ocean/Antarctic); 5. B – Platypus; 6. A – Ayr.

2 points for each correct answer.

Z₁	Q₂	U₃
A₄	Z₅	E₆
L	E	V₇

Z_1	Q_2	U_3
A_4	Z_5	E_6
L	E	V_7

Answer: VELAZQUEZ (Diego Velázquez, Spanish Baroque artist)

1 point for each correct answer, 5 bonus points for solving the snake.

Notes:
1. Jay-Z
2. In the James Bond series Q's real name is Major Boothroyd, Q standing for 'Quartermaster'
3. U Thant was the third Secretary General of the UN, from 1961 to 1971; he came from Burma
4. A1, A2, A3, A4 . . . etc.
5. The mark of Zorro
6. The River E
7. Abbreviation of Volt (named after Alessandro Volta)

1. D – Water and lava; 2. C – Hippocampus (from Greek 'hippos', meaning 'horse' and 'kampos', meaning 'sea monster'); 3. D – Brazil (the Brazilian flag has 27 stars); 4. A – Antonio (of whom Shylock demands a 'pound of flesh'); 5. B – Robert Catesby; 6. A – Bradley Cooper.

2 points for each correct answer.

1. Northumberland (Kielder Forest, 235 square miles); 2. Aspen; 3. Eucalyptus; 4. Carbon dioxide; 5. Cherry Orchard (Bournemouth's nickname, the Cherries, comes from the cherry orchard that grew around the location of their ground); 6. Willow; 7. Shed their needles; 8. Brazil; 9. Water; 10. Yew.

2 points for each correct answer.

MATCHING PAIRS: CHARACTERS IN LITERATURE

1C, 2H, 3G, 4L, 5B, 6J, 7K, 8D, 9A, 10F, 11E, 12I

1 point for each correct answer. If playing blind, i.e. without looking at the second set, 3 points for each answer.

MATCHING PAIRS: ANIMALS AND THEIR LATIN NAMES

1C, 2D, 3G, 4K, 5A, 6L, 7I, 8B, 9F, 10E, 11H, 12J

1 point for each correct answer. If playing blind, i.e. without looking at the second set, 3 points for each answer.

THE ANIMAL KINGDOM

1. Spider (gossamer is silk); 2. Emperor; 3. Cow; 4. Turkey; 5. Bat; 6. Electric eel; 7. Hare; 8. Kiwi; 9. Eight; 10. Tern.

2 points for each correct answer.

CHOICE OF FOUR 23

1. A – Canada (in a quirk of geography, the western tip of Canada's Ontario Peninsula between Lake Erie and Lake St Clair lies due south of Detroit, across the Detroit River); 2. D – More than two years; 3. A – Avian Flu; 4. D – Meet the Parents; 5. B – Emoji Dick; 6. D – Vanuatu.

2 points for each correct answer.

MONEY

1. The Rouble; 2. Sovereign; 3. Alexander Hamilton; 4. Hang Seng; 5. Mexican Peso; 6. Nick Leeson; 7. Switzerland; 8. 8 (hence was known as the 'piece of eight'); 9. Cartel; 10. Cryptocurrencies.

2 points for each correct answer.

CHOICE OF FOUR 21

1. B – Despacito (Luis Fonsi featuring Daddy Yankee); 2. A – F. Scott Fitzgerald; 3. C – Baku (28m below sea level); 4. B – Stormi; 5. D – Malala Yousafzai (awarded the prize in 2014 at the age of 17, along with Indian child rights activist Kailash Satyarthi); 6. D – A town (in the state of Jalisco in Mexico around 60 miles from Guadalajara).

2 points for each correct answer.

ODD ONE OUT 9

1. Banana – the others are types of tomatoes; 2. Winnipeg – the others are Great Lakes; 3. Susan Boyle appeared on Britain's Got Talent, the others were on The X Factor; 4. Barnaby Rudge is by Charles Dickens, the others are by George Eliot; 5. Crunchie is made by Cadbury, the others are made by Mars.

1 point for each correct answer, 2 bonus points for the correct reason.

CHOICE OF FOUR 19

1. A – Judge Doom (played by Christopher Lloyd); 2. C – Middlemarch; 3. C – 'Lose Yourself' (from the soundtrack of 8 Mile); 4. D – Papua New Guinea (Guinea pigs come from South America . . . Guinea, Guinea-Bissau and Equatorial Guinea are in West Africa, which is closer than Papua New Guinea, which is in Southeast Asia); 5. B – Soil; 6. D – Uruguay.

2 points for each correct answer.

FOOTBALL From page 104.

1. The UEFA European Championships (Euros); 2. Tottenham Hotspur (Sir Henry Percy 'Hotspur'); 3. The US; 4. Petr Čech; 5. Hamburg; 6. Christian Eriksen of Denmark; 7. Yugoslavia; 8. Ryan Giggs – 1999 (Bayern Munich), 2008 (Chelsea), 2009 and 2011 (Barcelona); 9. George Weah (Liberia); 10. Wembley Stadium (Tottenham, using it while their new stadium was being built, beat Arsenal 1–0 in the game).

2 points for each correct answer.

THE WISDOM OF THE CROWD: KEYS ON A PIANO From page 113.

There are **88** keys on the keyboard of a standard piano.

The Ministry takes the middle answer (the median) to represent the Crowd's collective answer, in this case it was 52 . . . the Crowd was out by 36. However, 88 was the most popular answer given by the Crowd.

If you guessed in the range 53 to 123, inclusive, you beat the Crowd!

Award points for accuracy as follows:
A guess between 79 and 97, inclusive, 2 points
Or a guess between 84 and 92, inclusive, 5 points
Or a guess of between 86 and 90, inclusive, 10 points

CITIES From page 79.

1. Zagreb (Croatia); 2. Gdańsk; 3. Melbourne; 4. Perth; 5. Karachi; 6. Florence; 7. Toyota; 8. Mexico City (at the Azteca Stadium in 1986, and previously in 1970); 9. St Petersburg (the Lakhta Center at 462.5m); 10. Stoke-on-Trent.

2 points for each correct answer.

THE ANCIENT WORLD From page 121.

1. The Olympic Games; 2. Pompey; 3. Sparta; 4. Emperors; 5. They were moved (60 metres higher to avoid being flooded by Lake Nasser after the construction of the Aswan Dam); 6. Plato; 7. Herodotus; 8. The Phoenicians (who passed it on to the Greeks); 9. The Hanging Gardens of Babylon; 10. Tunisia (modern-day Tunis).

2 points for each correct answer.

THE WISDOM OF THE CROWD: THE CHANNEL TUNNEL From page 98.

The Channel Tunnel is **31** miles long.

(The Channel Tunnel runs from Folkestone in Kent to Sangatte in France.)

The Ministry takes the middle answer (the median) to represent the Crowd's collective answer, in this case it was 46 . . . the Crowd was out by 15 miles.

If you guessed between 17 and 45, inclusive, you beat the Crowd!

Award points for accuracy as follows:
A guess between 28 and 34 miles, inclusive, 2 points
Or a guess between 29 and 33 miles, inclusive, 5 points
Or a guess of between 30 and 32 miles, inclusive, 10 points

CONNECTIONS 8 From page 97.

1. Walk; 2. Fish; 3. Dundee United; 4. Hummingbird; 5. The Elgin Marbles.

The connection is **cake** – cakewalk, fishcake, Dundee cake, hummingbird cake, marble cake.

2 points for each correct answer, 5 points for guessing the connection.

Answers in order of increasing difficulty:

Hamlet, Macbeth, Romeo and Juliet (1pt)
King Lear, Othello (2pts)
Titus Andronicus, Julius Caesar (3pts)
Antony and Cleopatra (4pts)
Timon of Athens, Coriolanus (5pts)

Honourable mentions: *Troilus and Cressida* is a 'problem play' with both tragic and comic elements, *Cymbeline* was originally classed by Shakespeare as a tragedy but some people regard it as a comedy. Do not award points for these, but neither deduct points.

Add up the points for the answers given, deduct 2 points for any incorrect answer.

1. The M25 (the motorway becomes an A road where it crosses the Thames Estuary at Dartford); 2. *Lady Chatterley's Lover*; 3. Fat Tuesday; 4. 'The Man Who Sold the World'; 5. The Berlin Wall; 6. Truro; 7. Orange; 8. North Korea; 9. Lewis Carroll; 10. Green; 11. Monkey puzzle (*Araucaria araucana*); 12. Billy the Kid; 13. Frogs' legs; 14. *Indiana Jones and the Last Crusade*; 15. Belgium.

2 points for each correct answer.

1. Selena Gomez
2. Cucumber
3. Kuala Lumpur

Award 5 points for a correct answer from the first clue only, 3 points from the first two clues, 2 points from the first three, 1 point if all four clues were needed.

2 Across: 1. Drake; 2. Chance; 3. *The Fall of the House of Usher*; 4. DMC (DeLorean Motor Company); 5. 'Mamma Mia'.

The link is 'RAPPERS': Drake, Chance the Rapper, Usher, Darryl McDaniels (aka DMC of Run-DMC), M.I.A. (Mathangi 'Maya' Arulpragasam).

4 Across: 1. Good (*The Good Wife, The Good Place*); 2. Black; 3. Dress down; 4. The Isle of Man; 5. The Thirteenth Amendment.

The link is 'FRIDAY': Good Friday, Black Friday, Dress Down Friday, Man Friday, Friday the Thirteenth.

1 Down: 1. WC (chemical formula for tungsten carbide, and abbreviation of water closet); 2. Strawberry; 3. Magnetic; 4. *The Killing*; 5. Mine (tin mines).

The link is 'FIELDS': W. C. Fields, Strawberry fields, Magnetic fields, *The Killing Fields*, Minefields.

3 Down: 1. Parallel; 2. The Central Line; 3. The New York Rangers; 4. Water; 5. Safari.

The link is 'PARK': Parallel park, Central Park, Park ranger, Water park, Safari park.

1 point for each correct answer, 2 bonus points for each correct link, 5 bonus points for solving the grid.

A$_1$	R$_2$	R
U$_3$	N$_4$	Y
Q$_5$	E$_6$	M

Answer: QUARRYMEN (John Lennon, Paul McCartney and George Harrison were members of the Quarrymen before they formed The Beatles.)

1 point for each correct answer, 5 bonus points for solving the snake.

Notes:
1. Indefinite article
2. Abbreviation of Rand
3. U-boat; Kretschmer was nicknamed 'Silent Otto'
4. K is used for King, so N is used for Knight
5. Its symbol is lower case q (its unit is coulomb)
6. Ecstasy

Answers in order of increasing difficulty (according to pubsgalore.co.uk, as of 2021):

Red Lion, Royal Oak (1pt)
White Hart, Crown (2pts)
Kings Arms, White Horse (3pts)
Plough, Ship (4pts)
Railway, Swan (5pts)

Add up the points for the answers given, deduct 2 points for any incorrect answer.

1. Newton Abbot; 2. J. K. Rowling; 3. Nerve; 4. Einstein; 5. Royal Mail Steamer; 6. *Pride and Prejudice*; 7. Chile and Argentina (5,308km); 8. Economist; 9. Four Yorkshiremen; 10. The International Space Station (ISS); 11. Big Boi; 12. Edinburgh ('Old Smokie'); 13. Nipples; 14. Dogs (The Queen's corgis); 15. Florence (it is in the Uffizi Gallery).

2 points for each correct answer.

1. B – W. H. Auden; 2. D – Tuscan (Tuscan is Roman, the others are Greek); 3. D – Mouse; 4. C – 5 minutes 55 seconds; 5. D – Wales; 6. B – Shooting Guard (Shooting Guard is basketball, the others are netball).

2 points for each correct answer.

1. King Cnut
2. Phosphorus
3. Haiti

Award 5 points for a correct answer from the first clue only, 3 points from the second clue, 2 points from the third clue, 1 point from the fourth clue.

There are **69** cities in the UK.

(Cities in the UK gain their status through Royal Charter. In the past, having a cathedral was the key criterion, but more recently the status takes account of other factors like population.)

The Ministry takes the middle answer (the median) to represent the Crowd's collective answer, in this case 60. The Crowd was out by 9.

If your guess was between 61 and 78, inclusive, you beat the Crowd!

Award points for accuracy as follows:

A guess between 62 and 86, inclusive,
2 points
Or a guess between 65 and 73, inclusive,
5 points
Or a guess between 68 and 70, inclusive,
10 points

ODDS AND ENDS 26 From page 178.

1. Dr Evil (from the Austin Powers films);
2. Athens 2004 (she won the 800m and
1,500m); 3. Mississippi; 4. Fort, castle,
stronghold or citadel; 5. *High Noon*;
6. Traffic lights; 7. 'Row, Row, Row Your
Boat'; 8. Tears; 9. A flooded river valley;
10. Michelle Obama; 11. Bread; 12. *Black
Panther*; 13. Margate; 14. Lafayette;
15. Sputnik.

2 points for each correct answer.

CHINA From page 171.

1. They were the first and last dynasties of
Imperial China (221 BC, 1644–1912); 2. The
Bird's Nest; 3. Dim sum; 4. Hong Kong;
5. Tea; 6. Grand Canal; 7. *The Manchurian
Candidate*; 8. Tennis (she won the 2011
French Open and the 2014 Australian
Open); 9. Rickshaw; 10. Red.

2 points for each correct answer.

PICTURE LOGIC: US STATES
From page 164.

A. New York	I. Kentucky
B. Louisiana	J. Pennsylvania
C. Washington	K. Missouri
D. Texas	L. Florida
E. Colorado	M. Nevada
F. Alaska	N. California
G. Oklahoma	O. Michigan
H. Massachusetts	P. Wyoming

1. C, F, N	3. K
2. D, N	4. C, P

5. A, C, F, O	11. I
6. H, L	12. B, D, L
7. P	13. J
8. H, K, O	14. E, P
9. A, G	15. M
10. E	16. H, J

2 points for each correct answer.

CONNECTIONS 11 From page 123.

1. Black; 2. The Darkness; 3. Persia;
4. Regent's Park; 5. Wales.

The connection is **princes** – The Black
Prince, Prince of Darkness, Prince of Persia,
Prince Regent, Prince of Wales.

2 points for each correct answer, 5 points
for guessing the connection.

CHOICE OF FOUR 22 From page 150.

1. A – Hippopotamus; 2. B – Lawrence
Dallaglio (85 points); 3. A – Drake ('God's
Plan'); 4. C – P. L. Travers; 5. A – Katherine
Schwarzeneggar; 6. A – Maine (the Quoddy
Head peninsula in Maine is the easternmost
point of the United States, about 3,154
miles from El Beddouza in Morocco).

2 points for each correct answer.

PUT IN ORDER 8 From page 142.

1. Uruguay (1930), West Germany (1954),
Brazil (1958), France (1998), Spain (2010)
2. *The Sound of Music* (1965), *The
Godfather* (1972), *Rocky* (1976), *The Deer
Hunter* (1978), *Raiders of the Lost Ark* (1981)
3. Lake Titicaca (8,372km²), Lake Erie
(25,744km²), Lake Michigan (58,000km²),
Lake Victoria (68,000km²), The Caspian
Sea (371,000km²)
4. Bears (appeared 38 million years ago),
Whales (50mya), Bees (100mya), Sharks
(350mya), Jellyfish (500mya)

3 points for each in the correct order.

LONDON UNDERGROUND STATIONS BEGINNING WITH 'L' From page 136.

Answers in order of increasing difficulty:

Leicester Square, Liverpool Street, London Bridge (1pt)
Lancaster Gate, Lambeth North (2pts)
Ladbroke Grove, Leyton, Leytonstone (3pts)
Latimer Road (4pts)
Loughton (5pts)

Add up the points for the answers given, deduct 2 points for any incorrect answer.

FOUR CLUES 8 From page 126.

1. RMS *Lusitania*
2. Prague
3. Smallpox

Award 5 points for a correct answer from the first clue only, 3 points from the first two clues, 2 points from the first three, 1 point if all four clues were needed.

CLUEDO ROOMS From page 104.

Answers in order of increasing difficulty:

Kitchen, Library, Lounge (1pt)
Conservatory, Study, Hall (2pts)
Dining Room, Billiard Room (3pts)
Ballroom (4pts)
Cellar (5pts)

Add up the points for the answers given, deduct 2 points for any incorrect answer.

FIFTY-FIFTY 9 From page 97.

1. New York (while Liberty Island is inside the state boundary of New Jersey, it is treated as an enclave of the state of New York); 2. Right; 3. Trees (there are around 3 trillion trees, versus around 100 billion stars). 4. Featherweight; 5. Yellow.

2 points for each correct answer.

MAGIC SQUARE 4 From page 120.

48	4	39a	3
36b	6	45	7c
8	44	-1d	43e
2	40f	11	.41

The Magic Number is 94. (5! = 120 (5 × 4 × 3 × 2 × 1), 4! = 24 (4 × 3 × 2 × 1), 2! = 2 (2 × 1).)

1 point for each correct answer, 5 points for finding the Magic Number.

Notes:
a. *The Thirty-Nine Steps*, by John Buchan.
b. 15 reds, 15 blacks, 6 colours.
c. Conrad Hilton Jr, Michael Wilding, Mike Todd, Eddie Fisher, Richard Burton (twice), John Warner, Larry Fortensky.
d. One under par, i.e. a score of -1.
e. According to the advertising slogan.
f. F-O-R-T-Y.

FIFTY-FIFTY 10 From page 112.

1. *The Lord of the Rings* (he's a hobbit); 2. Protestant; 3. The Atlantic (around 3.5 times more river water flows into it, much of the Pacific is bounded by the 'ring of fire', its coastline is typically mountainous and therefore lacking the large river basins that feed the other oceans); 4. Beyoncé; 5. Ten cents.

2 points for each correct answer.

ODDS AND ENDS 13 From page 88.

1. Hermitage; 2. Driver & Vehicle Licensing Agency; 3. Pickled Onion; 4. Denial; 5. Portsmouth (1939–46, the cup wasn't contested during the war); 6. Bognor; 7. Mali; 8. Haile Gebrselassie; 9. Stonehenge; 10. 'Top Scarer'; 11. King's Landing;

12. Stephen Hawking; 13. Penguin; 14. AGA cooker oven; 15. Nero.

2 points for each correct answer.

ODD ONE OUT 6 From page 79.

1. Geography – Nobel Prizes are awarded for the others; 2. Bucharest – the others all lie on the River Danube; 3. 20 – the others are represented by single letters in Roman numbers; 4. Richard Nixon resigned, the others died in office; 5. Bishop – the others are tales in Chaucer's *The Canterbury Tales.*

1 point for each correct answer, 2 bonus points for the correct reason.

WHAT COMES NEXT? 5 From page 72.

1. Mr. Brightside (last words of each line of the chorus of 'Mr. Brightside' by The Killers); 2. September (months with increasing number of letters); 3. King's Cross St Pancras (stops eastbound on the Circle Line from Edgware Road); 4. Brigadier (British army officer ranks in increasing seniority); 5. Carbon (elements in increasing order of atomic number).

3 points for each correct answer.

THE WISDOM OF THE CROWD: SHAKESPEARE PLAYS From page 67.

William Shakespeare wrote **37** plays.

The Ministry takes the middle answer (the median) to represent the Crowd's collective answer, in this case it was 20 ... the Crowd was out by 17. However, 37 was the most popular answer from women in the sample.

If you guessed between 21 and 53, inclusive, you beat the Crowd!

Award points for accuracy as follows:

A guess between 33 and 41, inclusive, 2 points
Or a guess between 35 and 39, inclusive, 5 points
Or a guess between 36 and 38, inclusive, 10 points

ODDS AND ENDS 9 From page 60.

1. *8 Mile*; 2. Cape Town; 3. The Fosse Way (Exeter to Lincoln via Bath); 4. Charles Darwin; 5. Mount Everest; 6. Jupiter; 7. Tetris; 8. *Hamilton: An American Musical*; 9. Captain America; 10. Anchor; 11. Velcro (after Swiss inventor George de Mestral noticed the seeds attached to his clothes and his dog's fur, investigating under the microscope discovered the seeds had little hooks); 12. Mahjong; 13. Katniss Everdeen; 14. Japan; 15. Extraterrestrial life.

2 points for each correct answer.

ODD ONE OUT 4 From page 49.

1. Rosemary is a perennial (grows for more than a season), the others are annuals; 2. The Strait of Messina is within a single country (Italy, separating Sicily from the mainland), the others are bordered by different countries; 3. Franklin – was not a president of the US; 4. Ciambella is a type of bread, the others are pasta; 5. Fermanagh is a county in Northern Ireland, the others are in the Republic of Ireland.

1 point for each correct answer, 2 bonus points for the correct reason.

FOUR CLUES 3 From page 42.

1. The Men's 4 x 400m Relay
2. The Danube
3. Dwayne Johnson

Award 5 points for a correct answer from the first clue only, 3 points from the first two clues, 2 points from the first three, 1 point if all four clues were needed.

CHOICE OF FOUR 5 From page 34.

1. B – Elizabeth Bennet (*Pride and Prejudice*); 2. C – Morecambe and Wise; 3. A – Greenland; 4. B – No worries (or no trouble . . . as used in a song of the same name in *The Lion King*); 5. A – Steel; 6. D – Oslo.

2 points for each correct answer.

FLORA AND FAUNA From page 26.

1. Sunflower; 2. Chrysanthemum; 3. A woody stem; 4. Carnivorous; 5. Busy Lizzie; 6. A mushroom; 7. Snapdragon; 8. Planting seeds and bulbs (it makes a hole in the soil); 9. They produce seeds, i.e. they are flowering; 10. Belladonna (Deadly Nightshade).

2 points for each correct answer.

THE ORCHESTRA From page 19.

1. Oboe (it keeps its tune better than, say, a stringed instrument); 2. Everybody plays; 3. Trumpet; 4. Concerto; 5. Wagner; 6. Simon Rattle; 7. Philharmonic; 8. Grieg (Piano Concerto in A minor); 9. 'Nimrod'; 10. Cello.

2 points for each correct answer.

WHAT COMES NEXT? 1 From page 11.

1. Hawaii (the last five US states to join the Union in order of joining, Hawaii being the most recent); 2. Ralph Fiennes (actors playing M in James Bond films in order of their first appearance); 3. Istanbul (names of Istanbul towards the present day); 4. J.M.W. Turner (people appearing on the Bank of England £20 note, towards the present day); 5. CP, also accept KP (initials

of the wives of Henry VIII . . . Catherine of Aragon, Anne Boleyn, Jane Seymour, Anne of Cleves, Catherine Howard, Catherine Parr).

3 points for each correct answer.

ODDS AND ENDS 1 From page 3.

1. Defeat Muhammad Ali; 2. Both drawn/painted by 'Leonardo' (Leonardo da Vinci/*Mona Lisa*, Leonardo DiCaprio/*Titanic*); 3. Yesterday; 4. The Seven Sisters; 5. The Order of Merlin; 6. Minneapolis; 7. CML; 8. Ebola Virus; 9. Car number plates; 10. Monsters University; 11. *Richard II*; 12. Flood; 13. The first book sold on Amazon.com; 14. Will Scarlet; 15. Carbonara.

2 points for each correct answer.

MAGIC SQUARE 6 From page 177.

1_a	14	14	4_b
11_c	7	6_d	9_e
8	10	10	5_f
13_g	2_h	3_i	15_j

Notes:

a. Although a prolific writer of poetry and plays, *The Picture of Dorian Gray* (1891) was Wilde's only novel.

b. Alabama, Alaska, Arizona, Arkansas.

c. 2017 hit by Luis Fonsi and Daddy Yankee.

d. Carmit Bachar, Ashley Roberts, Nicole Scherzinger, Jessica Sutta, Melody Thornton and Kimberly Wyatt (the main line-up, from their debut in 2003 until 2008).

e. 1996 film directed by Anthony Minghella starring Kristin Scott Thomas and Ralph Fiennes.

f. Shahada (Profession of Faith), Salat (Prayer), Zakat (Almsgiving), Sawm (Fasting), Hajj (Pilgrimage).

g. Chinese for 13, pronounced 'shi san', considered a lucky number in China.
h. From the Bingo call.
i. Red, Yellow, Blue.
j. Five permanent and ten temporary.

The Magic Number is 33. LPs play at 33 (and a 1/3) revolutions per minute.

2 points for each correct answer, 3 points for the magic sum.

FAMOUS PAINTINGS From page 171.

Answers in order of increasing difficulty:

Mona Lisa (Da Vinci) (1pt)
The Starry Night (Van Gogh), *The Last Supper* (Da Vinci), *The Scream* (Munch) (2pts)
Girl with a Pearl Earring (Vermeer), *Guernica* (Picasso), *The Birth of Venus* (Botticelli) (3pts)
The Night Watch (Rembrandt), *The Persistence of Memory* (Dalí) (4pts)
Whistler's Mother (Whistler) (5pts)

Add up the points for the answers given, deduct 2 points for any incorrect answer.

CHOICE OF FOUR 24 From page 163.

1. A – Apple; 2. C – The Style Council; 3. B – Japan (Aomori City in Honshu averages 8 metres of snow annually); 4. B – Benching; 5. B – Cobalt (kobold); 6. A – The Americas Cup (first awarded in 1851 when the Royal Yacht Squadron invited the New York Yacht Club to compete in a race around the Isle of Wight).

2 points for each correct answer.

FIFTY-FIFTY 13 From page 146.

1. Sea cucumbers; 2. Capulet; 3. Triassic; 4. Brazil; 5. Rihanna.

2 points for each correct answer.

MORE, LESS OR THE SAME? 5 From page 149.

1. The same – they each have one border (with Germany and Spain respectively).
2. Beatrix Potter Tales – 23 (21 Famous Five stories).
3. The same – 8 gallons in a bushel and 8 pints in a gallon.
4. Two US states, Alaska and Hawaii, border no other states (Maine is the only state that borders only one state).
5. Ayrton Senna died at the age of 34 (Alexander the Great was 33 when he died).

3 points for each correct answer.

ODDS AND ENDS 21 From page 141.

1. Blackcurrants; 2. *Brick Lane*; 3. *Dick Whittington*; 4. Kidderminster; 5. 18 / treble six; 6. Robert Maxwell; 7. *JFK*; 8. China clay; 9. Captain Tom Moore ('You'll Never Walk Alone' with Michael Ball); 10. Thabo Mbeki; 11. Leeds; 12. *The Red October*; 13. Sydney Harbour Bridge; 14. 'I Gotta Feeling' (Black Eyed Peas); 15. Newmarket.

2 points for each correct answer.

ODDS AND ENDS 20 From page 135.

1. Maria Mutola (of Mozambique); 2. Middlesbrough; 3. Flowers; 4. Sydney Opera House; 5. *Up*; 6. Africa; 7. He won Best Actor in consecutive years (1994/1995); 8. Asia; 9. Montserrat Caballé; 10. Spider-Man; 11. Sea levels; 12. The Berlin Wall; 13. Hall; 14. Nightmare; 15. *Goodfellas*.

2 points for each correct answer.

ABUNDANT CHEMICAL ELEMENTS
From page 125.

Answers in order of increasing difficulty:

Hydrogen (most abundant), Oxygen (third most abundant) (1pt)
Carbon (fourth), Nitrogen (sixth) (2pts)
Iron (ninth), Helium (second) (3pts)
Silicon (eighth), Magnesium (seventh) (4pts)
Neon (fifth), Sulphur (tenth) (5pts)

Add up the points for the answers given, deduct 2 points for any incorrect answer.

CHOICE OF FOUR 18 From page 119.

1. A – *Tess of the d'Urbervilles*; 2. C – Goldfinger (Ernő Goldfinger); 3. D – Oxford; 4. C – Posh; 5. A – Soil; 6. C – Michael Schumacher.

2 points for each correct answer.

CONNECTIONS 10 From page 112.

1. Black Cats; 2. Jonah; 3. Macbeth; 4. *The Thieving Magpie*; 5. 13.

The connection is **bad luck symbols** – Black cat, Jonah (a 'Jonah' is a jinxed person), *Macbeth* is considered an unlucky play, Magpie, the number 13.

2 points for each correct answer, 5 points for guessing the connection.

ALIASES From page 103.

1. Louis Armstrong; 2. Wonder Woman; 3. Frodo Baggins; 4. PewDiePie; 5. Heisenberg; 6. Caravaggio; 7. Fuzzy; 8. Stormy Daniels; 9. Billie Eilish (her full name is Billie Eilish Pirate Baird O'Connell); 10. *The Adventures of Tintin* (by Hergé).

2 points for each correct answer.

LETTER BOX 3 From page 89.

N	G_1	A
I_2	E_3	P_4
S_5	R	O

Answer: SINGAPORE

1 point for each correct answer, 5 bonus points for solving the snake.

Notes:
1. The MCG, known locally as 'The G'.
2. A square number will always be positive; a square root of a negative number is impossible. This doesn't trouble mathematicians who call it an imaginary number and represent it with a lower case 'i'.
3. Energy.
4. For piano.
5. Second.

CHOICE OF FOUR 15 From page 102.

1. B – John; 2. A – The Chainsmokers ('Closer'); 3. C – Dorset; 4. C – Marmite (banned because of the number of added vitamins and minerals); 5. B – Crotchet; 6. B – 400 metres.

2 points for each correct answer.

MAGIC SQUARE 3 From page 87.

13_a	2_b	9	4_c
2_d	11	6_e	9
5_f	10	1_g	12
8_h	5	12_i	3

The Magic Number is 28.

1 point for each correct answer, 5 bonus points for finding the Magic Number.

Notes:

a. Representing the 13 colonies.

b. A nickel is 5 cents, a dime is 10 cents.

c. In Buddhism there are four Noble Truths – pain, origin of pain, end of pain, path that leads to the end of pain.

d. Two stars orbiting each other.

e. $3! = 1 \times 2 \times 3 = 6$.

f. Chico, Harpo, Groucho, Gummo and Zeppo.

g. *The Red Vineyard* is believed to be the only painting Van Gogh sold in his lifetime.

h. 'It's All Over Now', 'Little Red Rooster', 'The Last Time', '(I Can't Get No) Satisfaction', 'Get Off of My Cloud', 'Paint It Black', 'Jumping Jack Flash', 'Honky Tonk Women'.

i. The dodecagonal £1 coin was introduced in 2017.

THE SOVIET UNION From page 75.

1. Leningrad; 2. Mikhail Gorbachev; 3. A star; 4. Germany (in 1939); 5. An Iron Curtain; 6. *The Hunt for Red October*; 7. Armenia; 8. Strategic Arms Limitation Talks; 9. Czechoslovakia; 10. 'Back in the USSR' (The Beatles).

2 points for each correct answer.

ODD ONE OUT 5 From page 72.

1. Benzidine is a compound, the others are elements (specifically halogens); 2. Dua Lipa is her real name, the others are stage names; 3. George I is in the House of Hanover, the others are Stuarts; 4. *Mister Magnolia* is by Quentin Blake, the others are by Roald Dahl (and illustrated by Quentin Blake); 5. Cricket – the others are Olympic sports.

1 point for each correct answer, 2 bonus points for the correct reason.

AIRPORTS From page 65.

1. Gatwick; 2. France (Paris Orly); 3. Port Stanley (The Falkland Islands); 4. Tokyo; 5. O'Hare; 6. Dubai; 7. Phoenix; 8. Ronald Reagan; 9. Albania (Tirana); 10. London Heathrow and New York JFK.

2 points for each correct answer.

FIFTY-FIFTY 6 From page 58.

1. York (Lancaster is Red); 2. Suez (193km, the Panama Canal is around 65km); 3. Turtle (voiced by Andrew Stanton, who also directed both films); 4. Southern Hemisphere; 5. Cake (in the UK, VAT is payable on biscuits but not cakes. The Inland Revenue asserted that Jaffa Cakes were biscuits and therefore tax was payable on them, but McVitie's won the verdict of the 1991 tribunal and the status of the Jaffa Cake as a cake was assured).

2 points for each correct answer.

CURRY From page 49.

1. Lentils; 2. Ghee; 3. 'Vindaloo'; 4. Rice; 5. Cauliflower; 6. Lamb; 7. Chicken; 8. Dopiaza; 9. Potato and spinach; 10. Chennai.

2 points for each correct answer.

CHOICE OF FOUR 6 From page 41.

1. B – Yellow; 2. B – Boardwalk; 3. A – Energy; 4. D – Bruno Tonioli; 5. B – Catherine Earnshaw (of Heathcliff in *Wuthering Heights*); 6. D – Great-grandson (Louis XIV reigned for 72 years and 110 days).

2 points for each correct answer.

CONNECTIONS 3 From page 33.

1. Tribute; 2. Kingfisher; 3. Bass; 4. Abbot; 5. Corona.

The connection is **beer** – the answers are all brands of beer.

2 points for each correct answer, 5 points for guessing the connection.

FIFTY-FIFTY 3 From page 26.

1. Sullivan; 2. Red; 3. Isle of Man (it is 572km^2, the Isle of Wight is 380km^2); 4. Zip (the zip was invented in 1891 called a 'clasp locker', the name zipper first appeared in 1923; Velcro was invented in 1955); 5. Elon Musk.

2 points for each correct answer.

IN COMMON 1 From page 18.

1. They are all seas; 2. Words that combine with countries to make film titles – *American Hustle, The French Connection, The Italian Job, The Spanish Prisoner, The English Patient*; 3. Adjectives in the titles of Dickens's novels – *The Old Curiosity Shop, Little Dorrit, Our Mutual Friend, Hard Times, Great Expectations*; 4. Their names are palindromes; 5. They join with words for meals to make phrases – *Naked Lunch*, high tea, dinner jacket, Last Supper, continental breakfast.

3 points for each correct answer.

MORE, LESS OR THE SAME? 1 From page 21.

1. The same – there is one carbon atom in each molecule (CO and CO_2).
2. Germany has 9 borders (France has 8).
3. The same – they were both 36 when they died.
4. A Pavarotti (£10 – a tenner/tenor; a deep-sea diver is £5, rhyming slang for 'a fiver').
5. Little Mix have 5 (One Direction have 4, as of 2021).

3 points for each correct answer.

COUNTRIES BORDERING BRAZIL From page 2.

Answers in order of increasing difficulty:

Argentina (1pt)
Colombia, Venezuela, Uruguay, Peru (2pts)
Bolivia, Paraguay (3pts)
Guyana, French Guiana (4pts)
Suriname (5pts)

Add up the points for the answers given, deduct 2 points for any incorrect answer.

FIFTY-FIFTY 16 From page 176.

1. School (a shoal is social group of fish); 2. The Missouri (at 2,341 miles is the longest river in the US, the Mississippi is only slightly shorter at 2,320 miles); 3. Hand (4 bones in each hand, the equivalent of metatarsals in the feet); 4. West Berlin (was a political enclave in East Germany); 5. Stalagmite.

2 points for each correct answer.

CONNECTIONS 15 From page 170.

1. Calculus; 2. Plum; 3. Brussels sprout; 4. Indiana Jones; 5. Green (for St Patrick's Day).

The connection is **professors** – Professor Calculus (in the Tintin stories), Professor Plum (in Cluedo), Professor Sprout (in the Harry Potter series), Indiana Jones is a professor of archaeology, Professor Green (the musician).

1 point for each correct answer, 5 points for the connection.

FOUR CLUES 10 From page 162.

1. 1986
2. Toronto
3. George Harrison

Award 5 points for a correct answer from the first clue only, 3 points from the first two clues, 2 points from the first three, 1 point if all four clues were needed.

MAGIC SQUARE 5 From page 155.

23$_a$	6$_b$	15	4
8$_c$	11$_d$	16	13
9$_e$	20$_f$	1	18
8	11	16	13$_g$

The Magic Number is 48 (its divisors are 1, 2, 3, 4, 6, 8, 12, 16, 24, 48).

1 point for each correct answer, 5 bonus points for finding the Magic Number.

Notes:

a. 1–20 are single numbers on the board, 21 can be scored with treble 7, 22 is double 11.

b. Hawaii, Alaska, Pacific, Mountain, Central and Eastern.

c. Noah, Shem, Ham, Japheth and their wives.

d. 'Legs eleven' as in the Bingo call.

e. According to Dante's *Inferno*.

f. *Bravo Two Zero*, a book by Andy McNab.

g. Argentina, Bolivia, Brazil, Chile, Colombia, Ecuador, French Guiana, Guyana, Paraguay, Peru, Suriname, Uruguay, Venezuela.

PUT IN ORDER 5 From page 84.

1. Pussy Galore, *Goldfinger*; Tiffany Case, *Diamonds are Forever*; Melina Havelock, *For Your Eyes Only*; Pam Bouvier, *Licence to Kill*; Xenia Onatopp, *GoldenEye*.
2. Pluto (2,377km in diameter), Ganymede (Jupiter's largest moon, 5,268km), The Sun (1.4 million km), Betelgeuse (1.2 billion km), The Crab Nebula (5.5 light years).
3. Snake Eyes (Pair of aces), Huey, Dewey, and Louie (Three of a kind – three twos, i.e.

three ducks), Broadway (Straight – AKQJ10 in different suits), Golf Bag (a flush in clubs), Four Horsemen (Four kings).
4. Jamaica (10,991km²), Iceland (103,000km²), Ivory Coast (322,463km²), Turkey (783,562km²), Mexico (1,964,375km²).

3 points for each in the correct order.

IN COMMON 10 From page 140.

1. Movies with punctuation in the title;
2. Become UK place names by adding 'Regis' (Lyme Regis, Grafton Regis, Milton Regis, Brompton Regis, Bere Regis); 3. All terms related to cricket; 4. Words containing hidden animals (rat, ape, fox, bat, cow); 5. Landlocked countries.

3 points for each correct answer.

TECHNOLOGY From page 134.

1. Kevlar; 2. Volvo; 3. Esperanto; 4. Porcelain toilet; 5. Universal Serial Bus; 6. Rosalind Franklin; 7. India (Mars Orbiter Mission, Mangalyaan, reached Mars orbit in September 2014); 8. Mercedes (Benz); 9. LG; 10. Debugging.

2 points for each correct answer.

IN COMMON 8 From page 125.

1. Movies with army ranks in their titles;
2. Add 'New' to each to make a US state;
3. People who have appeared on the Bank of England £5 note; 4. Artists who have hit songs with the word 'money' in the title ('Money', 'Money, Money, Money', 'Money (That's What I Want)', 'Money for Nothing', 'Money's Too Tight (to Mention)'; 5. Their capital cities all take the name of the country – Kuwait City, Mexico City, etc.

3 points for each correct answer.

1. $3 \times 5!$ is $3 \times (5 \times 4 \times 3 \times 2 \times 1)$, thus 360 ($3^5$ is 243).
2. Hercule Poirot appears in 33 novels (Miss Marple in 12).
3. Apartheid ended in 1990 (the Maastricht Treaty was signed in 1992).
4. Tupac Shakur was 25 (Buddy Holly only 22).
5. Red stripes – 7 (there are 6 white stripes).

3 points for each correct answer.

1. Bette Davis
2. Arsenal FC
3. 2000

Award 5 points for a correct answer from the first clue only, 3 points from the first two clues, 2 points from the first three, 1 point if all four clues were needed.

1. Double 3 (at the very bottom of the dartboard); 2. The Shannon (in Ireland, is 360km, 6km longer than the River Severn); 3. Ferns; 4. Trotter (James Trotter/Del and Rodney Trotter); 5. Duck-billed platypus; 6. Fermat's Last Theorem; 7. Rugby union (contested between Australia and New Zealand); 8. Valentines; 9. *Superman* (1978); 10. The London Underground; 11. Undersea (Untersee); 12. Pennsylvania; 13. Barbara Cartland; 14. The Scarecrow; 15. Aberdeen (AB).

2 points for each correct answer.

1. B – *King Lear* (said by Lear); 2. C – He is disqualified; 3. A – Australia; 4. C – East Sussex; 5. C – 'Punk Rock'; 6. B – Microwave oven.

2 points for each correct answer.

1	4a	7
8b	5	2
6c	9	3d

Notes:
a. St Louis (1904), Los Angeles (1932, 1984), Atlanta (1996). Los Angeles due to host for a third time in 2028.
b. Mercury, Venus, Earth, Mars, Jupiter, Saturn, Uranus, Neptune. Pluto is no longer classed as a planet.
c. Grumpy, Doc, Happy, Bashful, Sneezy and Sleepy, i.e. all except Dopey.
d. Tin.

2 points for each correct answer.

1. Adjectives in cocktails (Old Fashioned, Rusty Nail, Salty Dog, Dirty Martini, Bloody Mary); 2. All had countries named after them – China, The Philippines, Saudi Arabia, Columbia, Bolivia; 3. London streets (Savile Row, Brick Lane, Abbey Road, King's Road, Baker Street); 4. The world's most expensive living artist. The chronological record for the most money paid for a specific work by a living artist; 5. Places where Shaggy denied being caught in the chorus of 'It Wasn't Me'.

3 points for each correct answer.

CLUEDOKU 2 From page 58.

4_a	9	6_b
3	1	7_c
5_d	8_e	2

Notes:

a. 12 April 1861 to 9 May 1865.

b. Catherine of Aragon, Anne Boleyn, Jane Seymour, Anne of Cleves, Catherine Howard, Catherine Parr.

c. In order of population: Jersey, Guernsey, Alderney, Sark, Hem, Jethou, Brecqhou.

d. *Slaughterhouse-Five* by Kurt Vonnegut.

e. Peter Phillips, Zara Tindall, Prince William, Prince Harry, Princess Beatrice, Princess Eugenie, Lady Louise Windsor, James, Viscount Severn.

2 points for each correct answer.

ODDS AND ENDS 7 From page 48.

1. Reality; 2. 'Everything's going Jackanory' ('Country House', Blur); 3. *The Shining* (Stephen King); 4. Anglesey; 5. Rice; 6. They start and end with the same letter (Warsaw, Oslo, Addis Ababa); 7. Hedwig; 8. Be Right Back; 9. Their currency is francs (the Euro was adopted in 2002); 10. Blue; 11. Tequila; 12. Lady Gaga; 13. Four – Tony Blair, David Cameron, Theresa May, Boris Johnson; 14. Greenland; 15. 88.

2 points for each correct answer.

KARAOKE ESPERANTO 1 From page 40.

1. 'Don't Stop Me Now', Queen ('Two hundred degrees/That's why they call me Mr Fahrenheit'); 2. 'Fight for Your Right (to Party)', The Beastie Boys ('You've got to fight/For your right/To party'); 3. 'Only Girl (in the World)', Rihanna ('Want you to make me feel/Like I'm the only girl in the world'); 4. 'Baby One More Time', Britney Spears ('Oh, baby, baby/How was I supposed to know?'); 5. 'Ice Ice Baby', Vanilla Ice ('Check out the hook while my DJ revolves it/Ice Ice Baby').

3 points for each correct answer.

WHAT COMES NEXT? 3 From page 45.

1. Giga (increasing orders of magnitude greater than one); 2. Chilled (. . . On Sunday . . . activities on each day of the week from '7 Days' by Craig David); 3. 17 (seventeen – the numbers have increasing numbers of letters); 4. Duke (ranks in the Peerage in increasing seniority); 5. Sweden (European countries in order of area, decreasing).

3 points for each correct answer.

LINKOPHILIA 1 From page 24.

2 Across: 1. *Countdown*; 2. Grand; 3. Jack Straw; 4. *Curtain*; 5. ¼ (a quarter).

The link is 'FINAL': Final countdown, Grand final, Final straw, Final curtain, Quarter-final.

4 Across: 1. Silver; 2. A proof; 3. Train; 4. Hole; 5. A rubber.

The link is 'BULLET': Silver bullet, Bullet-proof, Bullet train, Bullet hole, Rubber bullet.

1 Down: 1. Ivory tower; 2. 'Gold' (by Spandau Ballet); 3. Jurassic; 4. Guard; 5. Mosquito.

The link is 'COAST': Ivory Coast, Gold Coast, Jurassic Coast, Coastguard, *The Mosquito Coast*.

3 Down: 1. Liberty; 2. Love; 3. 1,000; 4. Hops (hop plant); 5. The Prince of Wales.

The link is 'ISLAND': Liberty Island, *Love Island*, Thousand Island (dressing), Island-hop, Prince of Wales Island.

1 point for each correct answer. 2 bonus points for each correct link. 5 bonus points for solving the grid.

CLUEDOKU 1 From page 18.

2	9_a	8_b
7_c	3	1
5_d	4	6

Notes:

a. 10–19 July 1553, aka The Nine-Day Queen.

b. 'Some Might Say', 'Don't Look Back in Anger', 'D'You Know What I Mean', 'All Around the World', 'Go Let It Out', 'The Hindu Times', 'Lyla', 'The Importance of Being Idle'.

c. *Adam Bede*, *The Mill on the Floss*, *Silas Marner*, *Romola*, *Felix Holt, The Radical*, *Middlemarch*, *Daniel Deronda*.

d. The Saffir–Simpson hurricane wind scale categorizes tropical storms according to wind intensity; a Category Five hurricane has sustained wind speeds of at least 157 miles per hour.

2 points for each correct answer.

ODDS AND ENDS 2 From page 10.

1. 'The cold never bothered me anyway' (from 'Let it Go' from *Frozen*); 2. Africa; 3. West Ham United; 4. Berlin; 5. Leaning Tower of Pisa; 6. Acid; 7. *Three Men in a Boat* (by Jerome K. Jerome); 8. Too Long; Didn't Read; 9. The Warsaw Pact; 10. El Greco; 11. Kellogg's Corn Flakes; 12. Puritans; 13. Centre; 14. The Golden Gate Bridge; 15. Sandra Oh.

2 points for each correct answer.

MORE, LESS OR THE SAME? 6 From page 176.

1. The same – they both have 7 cervical vertebrae, the giraffe's are greatly elongated.
2. 4-letter names (there are five: Gold, Iron, Lead, Neon, Zinc; there are four with 5-letter names: Argon, Boron, Radon, Xenon).
3. 999 (CMI is the Roman numeral for 901).
4. Julius Caesar (Caesar was 56 when he died, Kennedy was 46).
5. Woodwind (6 woodwind, 4 brass).

3 points for each correct answer.

FIRSTS From page 2.

1. *Casino Royale*; 2. Harry Truman; 3. Reach the summit of Mount Everest; 4. First female jockey to win the Grand National; 5. Prime Minister; 6. *Gone with the Wind*; 7. First ever World Cup goal; 8. Australia; 9. Sherlock Holmes; 10. Swim the English Channel.

2 points for each correct answer.

PICTURE CREDITS